A KINGDOM FOR THE HEART

A timely retelling of an ancient epic

A KINGDOM FOR THE HEART

A timely retelling of an ancient epic

Case Stromenberg

*I've been searching for a heart of gold
And I'm getting old.*
\- Neil Young

iUniverse, Inc.
New York Bloomington

A Kingdom for the Heart
A timely retelling of an ancient epic

iUniverse books may be ordered through booksellers or by contacting:

iUniverse
1663 Liberty Drive
Bloomington, IN 47403
www.iuniverse.com
1-800-Authors (1-800-288-4677)

ISBN: 978-1-4401-3191-2 (pbk)
ISBN: 978-1-4401-3192-9 (ebk)

Printed in the United States of America

iUniverse rev. date: 3/30/2009

For Deborah, Mark, and Anna

Table of Contents

Preface

A very popular song in my younger days said "I've been searching for a heart of gold, and I'm getting old." This lyric expresses what this book is about as it traces an ancient epic story that looked for "a kingdom for the heart." That realm took many centuries to come into being and then became lost or at least was not very obvious. I had searched for it before but because of new hardships, I had a need to find it again.

This was not just a private matter. There were some major issues involved. By way of an illustration, let's say someone wants to investigate a new book about cinematic film that turns out to be just pages and pages of technical facts: all about the inventions that made motion pictures possible, stuff about camera work, set-ups for sound and lighting, and all the latest advances in digital imaging. The newfound book does a great job of presenting the technology and technique of film, but it misses a really important item, namely, *the story*. Absent from that volume of cinematic techniques are the actual movies and why they were made, artistic trends and genres as these developed, together with the most influential productions and people.

Our advanced technological age tends to reduce life everywhere to matters of technique, chemistry, formula, and money to acquire the newer technologies or to profit from their popularity. The benefits of technology and science, as useful as they are, seem to distract us from our deepest needs, feelings, intuitions, and so we lose something of what it means to be fulfilled human beings. Technique and formula are great *tools*, and the creativity or sense of accomplishment is great for those who use them. We like our more impressive products so much that we quickly fall into the belief that we can't have a good life without them. But our tools can never replace our hearts. When applied without much genuine personal concern, empathy, relationship, or inspiration, they soon show their limits.

Sensing that there is something deeper to life, many people go searching for their own soul, for an empowerment that can help them from within. Such a search is commonly called a spiritual journey. I've noticed, however, that many of the spiritual options placed before today's searcher very much involve the use of … *techniques*. Contemporary spiritual conversation is often about how to do things in a particular way in order to get a certain benefit for oneself. The idea is that the more you do things as instructed, the better off you'll be. Forms of spirituality do often reflect the society they are in.

In itself, there's nothing wrong with a technique-oriented spirituality, and even this book makes use of some techniques of investigation and presentation. But it seems really ironic to be focusing on techniques when a person is searching for something deeper than a technique-filled world. For myself, I had come to want more of the story of life and less of the "how to."

One of my preferred writers, C.S. Lewis, and also my son's favorite author, J.R.R. Tolkien, both communicated to millions all over the globe something about interesting journeys through realms of technique that were evilly applied. They did so by inventing fictional quests that overlapped aspects of the ancient epic with the mood and images of Pagan or Medieval European cultures. That mixture made wonderfully entertaining stories that many of us have long enjoyed. The following quotation taken from the film script of Tolkien's book *The Lord of the Rings* seems to appreciate the kind of search we are speaking of:

History became legend,

legend became myth,
and some things that should not have been forgotten
were lost.

Lewis and Tolkien each gave their response to technique-centered modern life by writing very creative stories as part of a long epic. And like them, I set out to seek what got lost in life, not as an attempt to equal their wonderful efforts but simply for my own therapy, hoping to see if what I needed most was really there.

My search involved a set of ancient documents belonging to the so-called "Abrahamic traditions" (Judaism and Christianity, and Islam's revised version of these). Of course, organized religions also use these documents, as do religious cultures that support a certain political and social agenda. I was not impressed with religion, despite having been quite involved in it, and I never held it against anybody if they disapproved of my study of the old sources. I had become very disillusioned with many of the people, organizations, and politics of the Abrahamic religions. Yet, I wasn't ready to dismiss the whole thing. I believed that somewhere along the way something had gone very wrong with the good Abrahamic tradition. There still was, I knew or hoped, a precious core, a heart of gold — largely lost, but waiting there for someone to find.

It seemed a good idea to have a fresh look at the ancient sources in order to discern the *thread* in their stories, the *epic* in all these old writings, hidden as that had become amid millions of squabbles, theological interpretations, narrow agendas, and many strange applications. Maybe it was possible to take the sources seriously, to take pleasure in their epic story without getting caught up in either religious dogma or modern disdain. Was there truly an enjoyable story here of the creative scope of a Lewis or Tolkien, and could it provide a help and outlook on life without a reliance on techniques, religious or otherwise? I believed there was such a story and that it would be important to discover it.

So what I needed to do was to go back over the old

documents to get a fresh view of the whole forest, as it were, without pausing to investigate every tree. My work would be to try to trace the fascinating flow of life as the ancients began to notice it, the strong current of good sense among numerous confusing eddies, chaotic whirlpools, and stagnant inlets. To follow that strong current, I needed to allow the story to tell itself and just go with the flow of it. Setting aside the ongoing arguments of scholars about who wrote what and when and which document is the most reliable, I just needed to focus on the overall subject matter and see if there still was a heart of gold there.

To me, this was all about self-therapy, enjoyment, and discovering why so much of the various religions that have taken their start with Abraham, the religions that have the most adherents in the world, don't seem to be working very well. I've heard it said, "Religion is for those who want to escape hell, but spirituality is for those who have been there." That is probably a bit oversimplified but I thought it carried a powerful kernel of truth: those who look for real personal redemption and recovery can never for long be satisfied with taking part in religion but will instead seek newness from the inside out. Organized religion may be necessary and somehow be tied to personal spirituality — but it is certainly *distinct* from that.

Apprehensively, I made a start on my project, wondering how I would be feeling during the course of this search. Would I be happy to get close to a heart of gold, only mildly encouraged, cynical, devastated, or just continue questioning? The answer to that unfolds in this book.

The ancient epic is also still relevant to the violent and perennial conflicts in the Near or Middle East, involving people and nations who claim to be of Abraham. I made sure to deal with that relevance without having the volume become a commentary on the modern quarrels.

To seekers of any kind who are about to take up this book, I might suggest that you just relax and enjoy the long story. Keep on reading, past any troubling details, until you start to see the great forest in spite of the many trees — that is, until the wide panorama and full sweep of the epic becomes clear and stays with you.

Case Stromenberg
Alvinston, Ontario, December 2008

A Kingdom for the Heart

A timely retelling of an ancient epic

The old setting

Chapter One
The world of the epic

1. The plan

Mapping out a general plan to seek the epic and its heart, I picked up my equipment and began. I carried with me a moderate acquaintance with the ancient Hebrew and Greek of many of the old documents, and in my backpack was the study and work I had done previously in teaching history and theology. Besides these items, I brought to the search my strong dismay about religion and a personal knowledge of its weaknesses. These I would need in order to avoid getting side-tracked from my aim to find the epic and enjoy it, as well as my hope to discover a genuine Abrahamic spirituality.

The first challenge to face me on this journey was the task of removing the mental filters through which the stories of Earth's origins had been sifted, and I mean the modern filters, not the ancient ones. This was not easy. All my life, it seems, I heard at schools, colleges and elsewhere the criticizing ridicule that the old stories are "not scientific." I always found these attacks kind of silly and a little too arrogant: imagine writing off thousands of years of the development of humankind and civilization because the old way that people expressed things doesn't meet with modern approval! And then, I had also often heard the debate from the other side, namely, the adamant efforts of "Creation Science" people to say that the old sources contain verifiable information about the physical origins of the universe.

Well, maybe there was some truth in both sides of the debate but I found it very unfortunate that this ongoing argument has held the ancient sources hostage, both sides using or abusing them in a science controversy instead of letting the documents be quietly absorbed by thoughtful readers. The Genesis accounts of origins are *not* about the modern "creation-versus-evolution" issue at all. Rather, they form part of an introduction to the epic of Abraham and his descendants. Though I could see some evolution and some intelligent design (without committing to the emotion and ideology of either side), right from the start I had to acknowledge the *story* rather than the science debate. The documents were primarily the Abraham story, and that's the direction in which I needed to head.

I had to find and then retell something of the great significance that the Genesis accounts must have had for Abraham's family. These stories had an importance beyond myth to something truly legendary, influencing the family's beliefs and ways of living life. To uncover this and put it in modern words was a tall order, but it was the necessary start in the search for Abraham's kind of spirituality. Aside from any issue of doctrine, the ancient authors and composers seem to have known a deep meaning and sense of home within themselves, though the things they hoped for in life always lay outside, above, and in front. Though the story was indeed about things *out there,* its benefit was clearly personal, in their *heart and mind.* That sounds almost like a contradiction, but it's a great truth that tends to elude people. Yet by grasping it, some persons could turn away from the ever-moving mirage and disappointing dream of a present paradise and not give up their deeper hopes. They could leave the outer illusion without becoming disillusioned within, and that powerful outlook I began to see as being very much a part of the whole story.

My first steps in the journey of discovery were actually away from the book of Genesis. There was another very ancient belief that intelligent life existed in the universe long before it appeared on our world, and that there came a time when some of that life reached the planet unwillingly. These beliefs looked far back to an enormous event when the surface of an earlier Earth was much different from what it is now, back to an unknown distant era when the Highest Power in the universe was challenged by the hostility of a great subordinate. That lesser force, whatever it precisely was, apparently lost sight of its purpose and belonging, becoming obsessed with its own great potential. The subordinate hungered for more fame, for more fortune, and especially for *dominance*.

In effect, the Rival Power wanted to be in the position of the High Power, whom it blamed for the state of affairs that allowed no joint rule on an equal level. A hateful frustration possessed this Rival as it sought, but did not achieve, the ultimate supremacy it craved. Many creatures under its influence also darkened their thoughts to dwell on similar ambitions and they looked to the Rival, or Adversary, to pave the way to their goal.

According to this fascinating tradition, a minority of all the creatures in the distant universe joined the Rival in its bitter rebellion. Then two opposing sides faced each other, two armies of a kind never seen by people on Earth. In the great war that followed, the majority forces that were loyal to the High Power achieved the victory. Justice was then carried out and the Adversary with its cohort was launched far into the universe to be confined to a small planet. That little ball of rocks and gases proved to be a most dreary place, shrouded in a thick, foul haze that made it utterly dark, cheerless, and hostile to life.

There the whole matter might have ended for all eternity, but the thoughts of the High Power were most wise and could not be calculated for their number or depth. A strange plan began to put into effect: the rebels were not going to be granted full control of their place of exile. The dark little planet would be transformed into a most attractive, almost divine place, presided over by an almost divine creature with amazing potential. Through this exceptional being, the embittered Rival would be reminded that the remote planet would not be its stepping stone back to glory. Like a disgraced general given some limited freedom on a secluded island of exile, the Adversary would find its power so cleverly channeled that it would end up unwittingly serving the purposes of the victor.

I had my own questions about this kind of story but I decided that for the moment and probably for the duration of the whole search, a much better question would be: "Do I get it — am I enough into the story to like it and understand it?" Unlike much that I was taught in various schools, I had to go easy on analyzing everything and go big on just relaxing with the story. I had to give myself a real chance to become thoroughly re-acquainted with the epic. My aim had to be to get from the story what was there and to grasp its general flow. Analysis, if necessary, could come later. And that, I believed, was a pretty good approach to any set of writings, not only the ancient epic.

2. Development and challenge

Looking now at the Genesis account, I came to realize that it actually said next to nothing about the origins and development of the universe! Its focus was on Earth rather than the heavens, and the documents spoke of great changes on the planet itself. Let's see how that account goes, with a bit of elaboration inspired by other parts of the documents.

A very long time ago (how long ago it doesn't say), the surface of the little planet was shapeless and lifeless. Watery masses covered the place and its atmosphere was not air as we know it but thick layers of gaseous vapor and smoke that kept Earth in a constant state of darkness. Then, at some appointed moment, an enormous "Wind of Great Power" came upon the Earth. At first, this power from the Creator hovered warmly over the waters for a very long age, brooding upon them like a hen broods over the potential life underneath it until it is time for the life to appear. But at a divine command, the Great Wind mightily stirred the thick haze that blanketed the planet. More and more did the gloomy thickness move, and suddenly there was fierce lightning, first at one location, then gradually spreading to many places. The haze now grew less dense so that some light from above was able to filter through the heavy atmosphere. There was then a first day on the dark planet.

As the tremendous, world-wide storm continued to swirl, it made new combinations of matter, and so various gases were forming all over the globe. In this way, there grew a large expanse of air that came between the surface waters and the vapors above them, causing the two liquids to separate. The new air appeared to have the strength of pillars as the higher moisture was lifted upwards. Higher and higher moved the band of vapors until it became a sort of roof or "firmament," arching way above the planet.

The liquid mass covering the surface now began to be transformed. As the firmament rose up, the waters below it shrunk back steadily so that dry ground made its debut in the midst of the vast seas. The patient, creative brooding of the Great Wind suddenly bore visible fruit when the color of the land began to change from grey and red and brown to many hues of green, sprouting new life-forms of tender shoots, of spore plants, seed plants and fruit plants.

The mass of vapors higher up broadened out as they rose up, becoming dispersed and thinner until with time the skies began to clear. When this happened, a wonderful source of light was revealed, far above the firmament. A great yellow star shone on the planet for a short while and was periodically replaced by a smaller object of white radiance, along with innumerable tiny points of light. Now there clearly was day and night, and the possibility of tracking times and seasons.

The creative Great Wind, still moving on as it kept working by a hidden design, also brought life to the seas. The waters started teeming with life on the sea floor and also with swimming forms, both little and large. Neither was the air without life as numerous insects took flight and birds enjoyed their freedom. Later, to the land came burrowing things, creeping things and all sorts of small and large animals with four legs or two. These all were fruitful with their own kind so that they multiplied rapidly and spread over large portions of the developing planet.

This was the purposeful order in which the "Wind of Great Power" brought life to a once dead world.

3. *Discoveries on the day of tranquility*

When the creative work was well-advanced, the dark world was dismal no longer. The exiled Rival and its cohort, barely able to endure the change, kept to the more lifeless, waterless places on Earth and covered themselves with the hills and rocks. Chafing under the thought that even its little island in the universe would no longer bend under its forceful rule, the Adversary saw in the marvel of the new world a great threat, as if a good kingdom of created life was swallowing up the darkness. The Rival's shallow self-satisfaction blended with a deeper resentment, plain arrogance mixed with bitter loathing, and these vile expressions soon found a reason to grow still more intense.

One day, the Great Wind suddenly abated and soon seemed to vanish altogether. The immense disturbances in air and ground slowed down considerably and were far less frequent. An unusual but not unpleasant quiet now spread over the planet. Earth no longer heard or felt the massive creative activity it had become accustomed to. For the indefinite future, the planet would remain more or less what it was.

There was one last life-form that had been made just before the time of tranquility, though this newly-created thing seemed quite a disappointment for being at the climax of the remaking of the dead planet. In fact, it simply appeared to be a slight variation of some other earthly beings that had already existed. Just like these others, it had only two legs and no tail, was of no impressive size, carried a minor covering of hair, and was able to use a few simple tools. Least inspiring of all, there existed only two representatives of this special Earthling, a male and a female.

Nevertheless, despite their close resemblance to some other beings, the two were certainly special. They lived in a specially-designed large garden and possessed the power of an intricate and intelligent language, and those two things were quite unique among all the creatures now inhabiting the planet. The man and the woman tended to the great garden each day and studied various life-forms, the male having begun a practice of giving the names to the animals.

The newest creature, unimpressive in its outward appearance and gardening task, was potentially the ruler of the whole planet. Its language ability and especially the naming power indicated this possibility. In some way, the last creature shared the divine privilege to understand and influence what had been made. At least it had the ability to investigate and come to know many of the laws and secrets of the universe, and by implication to know some of the Creator's own mind and character. This was truly an awesome knowledge and strength.

As the Rival pondered all these things, it figured out what was indeed the truth, namely that the final creature was in some way a likeness of the High Power in the universe, and was destined to become both the chief worker and the ruling creative power on Earth. The ultimate triumph of the invasion of the dark planet therefore involved the success of this last being, a triumph that the Adversary could not afford to allow. To have been banished from the vast heavens was enough of a catastrophe to bear, but having another potentially-great ruler in the very place of exile was a maddening challenge that could not be tolerated.

To kill the final creature wasn't yet an option. The vigor of the High Power's life and likeness in this male and female would prevent that for now. So the Rival decided to go see for itself, to experience the last creature covertly, to test the strength of these two unique beings and find their weakness.

4. The great separation

I had to keep setting aside modern concerns about how factual the story was or how it has become attached to various religions. Applying some self-discipline to avoid stopping too long to analyze or find fault, I moved on to catch the sense and feeling of the stage that was being set as introduction to the epic story of Abraham. In my written notes, I embellished the ancient stories a little and combined their accounts, but otherwise I followed the old sources quite closely.

In the middle of the paradise where the last creatures lived, stood two large trees that were quite distinct from the other trees, as well as being different from each other. The First Tree was immensely tall and strong, its unchanging green peak always seeming to pierce the sky. It was a symbol of the enduring and noble life the man and woman would have if they continued in a relationship with their High Power.

The Second Tree, on the other hand, was a low, bushy fruit plant, intriguingly sporting a range of colors. This beautiful object had the disappointing habit of shedding its many fine leaves for several weeks at a time. Then the tree looked dead and forlorn, and in that way pictured the kind of futile existence the final beings would have if they chose to turn away from the High Power.

The visual lesson of the two special trees posed the options symbolically, starkly and clearly, and yet the man and woman did not understand their choice very well. What did they really know of the evil of going against the universal Power? The thought of doing any such thing had not even entered their minds. Rather than that, in the cooler part of each day they met happily with the Creator, conversing in the intricate language that had been planted in their memory. They also enjoyed a close relationship with each other, for though the man and woman were naked, they were always fully respectful and supportive of each other and had no experience of any shame.

Among the animals that they had observed there was the dragon, a serpentine reptile of moderate size, with four short legs and a covering of many subtle colors and skin designs, some of which cleverly changed to match its background and help hide it. One day, when the woman was near the Second Tree, she was startled to discover the camouflaged "serpent" in it. The snake-like thing spoke as soon as it was discovered, but this was no talking-animal story. The Rival had entered the body of the dragon in order to spy on the couple and lure them into a trap.

"Is it true," began the Adversary (not the serpent), "that the Power said you may not eat from any tree in the garden?" This was certainly not true and the woman, smartly enough, answered correctly that they had only been commanded to refrain from the fruit of the Second Tree, and if they ate of it, that would be the death of them.

"You are not sure to die," hissed the false voice in reply. "The Power knows that when you eat from this tree your eyes will be opened and you will be like God!"

Of course, she was already like God in some significant ways but the wily thing continued to reason with the woman this way, in due time winning her over. She now inspected the fruit on the tree closely and it became strongly attractive to her eyes, looking like irresistible food. The young woman was also intrigued with the suggestion that the tree would provide a quick and magical way to obtain supernatural insight, so she reached out her hand and plucked some of the unique fruit (certainly no apple!). Then she brought the man a sample and they both ate.

At first, there was nothing but the joy of eating, the fruit tasting sweet and delicious. How could anything so good be so bad? When it had been consumed, however, they began to feel a new sensation, something strange and awful. Soon they didn't feel so good about having eaten. The man and the woman looked at each other to see if they were both experiencing the same thing, and then they saw it! They were naked. Of course, each of them already knew what the other looked like, but now they felt vulnerable. Immediately they backed away and covered themselves with hands and nearby branches.

Not long thereafter, as the day grew cool again, the High Power came to talk with them as usual but they hid when he called. Finally they spoke up from their hiding places, saying that they were naked. "Where did you get this knowledge of shame and fear?" the Creator asked. "Have you eaten from the tree I forbade to you?"

"It was the woman you put me with," answered the male in

his own defense, putting the blame more on the Creator than on her, "she gave me the fruit and I ate it."

But the female blamed the dragon more than herself. "It tempted me, so I ate."

The High Power turned to the Adversary, cursed it and said, "I will put loathing between you and the woman, between those who follow her and those who follow you. The offspring of the woman will crush your head, though you will strike his heel."

Then the Power predicted that without the intended relationship, life for humans would often be unsuccessful and frustrating. Difficulty and pain would accompany the giving of birth and yet women would continue to long for husbands, while men would toil hard their whole lives to provide food and find the soil resisting their labors with weeds and hurtful nettles. In the end, the ground would cover both of them in death — "Dust you are and to dust you shall return." Futility would follow their best efforts, and hurt would be the price of fruitfulness or joy.

After the Power had left them and they were all alone, the man thought it best to take a position of authority over the woman with him. He called her *Havah*, a name we know as Ava, Eva, or Eve. It meant "Mother" because he now understood that she would be the origin of a special race to trample on the Adversary. The man's own name became *Adham* or Adam, a reference to red-brown color, perhaps of his naked skin or of his hair, like the hue of the soil he worked on.

The couple was not allowed to stay in the great garden where the two special trees stood and where their days had been uncomplicated. Now banished like the Rival, they began to roam the wild Earth, the territory the Adversary had thought was its own to rule. The human attempts at rulership now began.

5. The fate of the new exiles

People added to the already established population of shadowy exiles on the planet. The humans, trudging along with their unsettled feeling of enforced homelessness, often felt a rebellious reaction and were sometimes sympathetic to the Rival despite the hatred it had for their presence in the world. Seen in a different way, however, banishment proved to be a benefit to human development as they began a hunt for a new and possibly better homeland. This way, they might regain the hope that the garden represented and the new quest could give their lives meaning.

According to the tradition of the documents, these first people, appointed to be the Creator's representative rulers on Earth, went into exile eastward of the garden that lay in a region called Eden. The land was said to have been located beyond the place where the Tigris and Euphrates rivers join, and that would put it somewhere in the southern part of present-day Iraq, or perhaps now under water in the Persian Gulf. It is also possible that the joining of the two great rivers was formerly at a more northerly location, or maybe the term "joining" meant the nearness of the rivers to each other at their common source in the mountain springs. In any case, eastward from the junction of the rivers is where some or all members of the primeval family made their sad journey.

None of the documents tell us how far they traveled in the course of their reportedly long life, though some inhabitants of today's Sri Lanka believe that Adam's burial place is located on their island, which long ago used to be joined to the subcontinent of India. There has also been some guesswork that significant branches of the migration became the origins of culture in southern Mesopotamia and in Egypt, but that is only speculation. Whatever may have happened to that first family "made in God's image," it was said that the descendants did not all stay together but dispersed far and wide.

For many years, the image family would have carried within them the trauma of expulsion and broken trust. Though they maintained some knowledge of the High Power and a form of spirituality, they struggled with the harsh demands of survival outside of the great garden and with the ineffectiveness of many of their efforts, including what they tried in the way of worship.

Surely they would have suffered from their perplexity and inner pain, feeling acutely the hurt and loss of a secure home, of a lost identity and positive destiny. The tough outcome of the broken relationship and all of those awful consequences were passed on successively to each new generation. The traditional story therefore points to a significant fall of the humans, in spiritual or emotional terms at least, rather than the modern idea of a progressive rise.

The ancient sources suggest that it wasn't until after Adam had grandchildren (of which there were very many in his long life) that certain people were ready to try to restore the old special relationship. Accordingly, some men began to seek the High Power more intensely, and as they did, they would have found that if they altered their previous opinion that the Power was a hard-hearted being who punished severely every trifling error, there actually was great benefit in connecting with the divine. This spiritual discovery astounded them and they became changed people, soon developing in ways that exceeded the rest of the population as they became remarkably wise and creative. Other people stood in awe of their inspired gifts and strengths, and took to calling them "the Sons of God."

In their earlier years, the Sons of God tended to live apart from others, either alone or in small bands, but there came a time when some wanted to enjoy the companionship of women. So they came to the daughters of other men and chose wives from among them. The offspring of these unions were the product of two ways of life, and with their unique upbringing these children grew into influential leaders in society, making a great name for themselves in a variety of endeavors.

Yet there was a dark side to the success and greatness of the offspring, a troubling aspect that often became their undoing. They imagined themselves to be above the crowd, beyond the norms of behavior that governed ordinary human society. If other men had one woman, they could have more; though others were punished for crimes, they themselves could not be touched. As a result, several of the children of the Sons of God, in spite of some godly qualities, became evil. For this reason they were also known as *Nephilim,* or "The Fallen."

The era of the Sons of God and their direct offspring has no date but its mention was clearly meant to refer to a society that existed long before the "first" civilizations of Mesopotamia and Egypt. Over the course of this very ancient era, as many centuries came and went, it became apparent that in spite of the special powers, ingenuity, and good intentions seen among humankind, the race was seriously flawed and damaged. That negative fact became a significant part of the outlook of those who wrote the epic.

Violence and corruption spread through the world wherever people traveled and made a home, and it has been the common tradition of many different societies of later times that eventually a flood of uniquely huge proportions destroyed most of human life, ending much of the evil that had come to that very ancient human society. Indeed, the word "flood" is somewhat of a misnomer, for no seasonal inundation, no matter how heavy, can match the vast destruction and submersion of which these several old legends tell.

6. *Technology and human need*

A few generations after the huge submersion, an exceptional man of talent, will, and intellect, made a great name for himself. He was *Nimrod,* also known as "Enmer the Hunter" in Mesopotamian lore. This clever man skillfully figured out techniques for hunting game with great success, and this was very significant in the post-flood period when large game was still scarce. Now the instruction of the Creator to the human race had been to spread out over Earth's surface and become rulers over the whole planet, but, according to a certain story tradition, Nimrod was angry about the flood and told people they could learn better from him. He led them to focus diligently on their survival by having them construct citadels within their territories. Having already earned people's gratitude with his hunting skills, he came to rule the newly-built Mesopotamian strongholds as their overlord.

From the same story we learn that it was Nimrod who built the huge Tower of Babel as a way to outsmart God in case there was another great flood. The high structure was designed to exceed the height of any flood and it was made with burnt clay brick, cemented together with *bitumen*, tar, so as to be virtually waterproof. This Babel project at first successfully spread Nimrod's rebellious anxiety and kept people from following the mandate to spread out over the Earth. The great fame and security of the huge tower was beginning to make quite a name for its builders. Mysteriously, however, the work crews stopped communicating with each other, causing chaotic confusion. They brought construction on the tower to a halt and moved away in different directions.

It was becoming evident that if people were to do well on Earth they would need more than ambition, wits and strong leadership. They would also need to relate to each other well, though that required a deep healing and personal recovery, the development of a peaceful heart and spirit. There had to be something profound for the inner self, something beyond what Nimrod and his tower offered, something more than anger, ideology, and technology.

What was needed was a far-reaching transformation that matched the damage of broken trust and hurtful connections. Recovery of the human race could not be just a one-time event but had to be profoundly complete: an open acknowledgement of the problem, together with an appropriate settling of scores, capped off by a merciful rebuilding of peace. But a thorough restoration could not be understood by everybody, and in any case it could only be worked out over the span of many years, indeed of many generations. In contrast to the impatience and quick-fixes of our contemporary society, many ancients showed every indication of seeing life through a telescope rather than a microscope — that is, they took a much longer view of things.

The stories found in Genesis, and elsewhere in ancient

literature, formed the background and basic outlook of various people in that world, giving them a sense that life was about more than survival, luck, and getting ahead. There was a larger story here. There had been some major disruptions in the world and a start had to be made on a lengthy journey of renewal.

Consequently, it was time for the epic to begin.

A Kingdom for the Heart

A timely retelling of an ancient epic

The epic begins

Chapter Two
A unique quest

1. Hopes tried and lost

Dozens of centuries cast their long shadow on Earth while humans multiplied and spread out over the globe. Their accomplishments, often astounding, went far beyond tools for survival. Creativity of all kinds reflected their considerable powers but permanence escaped their grasp. Marvelous buildings and unbelievable monuments were erected by them and later stood as lonely sentinels, abandoned. Strong kingdoms and clever societies were developed and then were conquered and destroyed or simply decayed into forgotten ruins. Inspired works of art and music were hailed and exhibited before they crumbled into dust and disappeared into silence. Even when proud achievements seemed permanent and virtually invincible, a great fire, earthquake, flood, pestilence or human destruction would arrive to enforce a sadder humility.

The momentary visions that inspired people's many elusive quests for a new paradise were often nearly as short-lived as the old garden had been, but at least these recurring ideas and dreams showed that people were aiming for something much more in life than mere physical survival and natural existence. There was something about this race of creatures that was unique among all life on Earth.

The tragic cycles that people experienced also included their attempt at renewing themselves through contacting or placating the divine Power. This was more than a fear of natural forces or a hope for success in the hunt or in the growing of crops. It was all these things too but there was in addition a deep mental and emotional restlessness in the humans that needed a measure of quieting and calming satisfaction. Efforts to achieve greater inner peace led to the multiplying of shrines, priesthoods, and sacrificial rites — much of which, we note, had the smell of death, dread, guilt, and sadness.

Despite the difficulty of grasping the unseen and knowing the unknowable, individuals and societies continued their efforts at both inner and outer improvement. The gnawing lack of permanence or a secure paradise, together with the need for physical and social survival, produced all that we can now detect amid the sands and stones of their remaining monuments and homes. Human life was to continue developing in this wistful way, generation after generation.

2. The departure

In one particular very ancient century, there appeared the beginnings of a different approach to living. In Mesopotamia, shortly after 2000 BC, there lived a man called *Terach,* and what little we know specifically about him involves his migration from the south Sumerian city of Ur, not far from the Persian Gulf (some think it may have been another Ur, a good distance to the north in present-day Kurdistan). Terach moved to a place called *Charan* in what is now northern Syria. He had not intended to settle there because his voyage was supposed to end in the land of *Canaan,* today's region of Palestine, Israel, and southern Lebanon.

For some reason, Terach never completed his journey. Some traditions say he lost interest after he became wealthy by carving statuettes of household gods in the Syrian city, and maybe also he became endeared to Charan by its close similarity to the name of his deceased son *Haran* (possibly pronounced the same way as the city). At a certain time, however, two members of the family, namely Haran's son *Lot* and Terach's son *Abram,* pulled up their stakes and continued the long-delayed trek to Canaan. They arrived finally at a settlement called *Shechem,* a locality that we will hear much more about later.

Because millions of people now know of Abram (Abraham, Ibrahim) through their religion, I thought I should try to get

the young Egyptian woman *Hagar* (sometimes spelled as *Hajar*, from Arabic), became the means of Sarai having a baby. Hagar was given to Abram to sleep with and a son was born to them, but through a standard legal fiction the child was considered to have been of Abram and Sarai. He received the name *Ishmael*.

Eventually, however, Sarai herself, now known as *Sarah* in her advanced age, did manage to give birth after all. Her very own child was also a son, named *Isaac* (in Hebrew: *Yitschak*), but between the two boys and between their mothers friction developed. Of course, the hostility, taunting, and jealousy of that conflict is understandable considering the nature of Abram's marriage and family, but it is of special interest to us because the later tribes of Arabs were to claim descent from Ishmael (Arabic: *Ismail*) while the nation of Israel traced its ancestry to Isaac.

When Abram, agonizingly believing that God required it, nearly turned his son into a burnt sacrifice on a high place called Moriah (in what eventually became the site of Jerusalem), the Bible states that the boy was Isaac, while Islamic tradition insists it was Ishmael. In any event, though he was by no means a believer in human sacrifice, Abram's reluctant willingness to offer up his son to God showed how dedicated he was to letting go of the things that other men held onto as part of their dreams and hopes. In the end, he instead offered a substitute sacrifice, a male sheep that had gotten its horns stuck in the undergrowth.

Now whether we apply to Abram's deed the term adherence or faith or submission, his exceptional understanding and living of life was powerfully unique in his time and proved over the years to have been epoch-making. More than any other known person of his day, Abram resisted the urge to seek his own way to a personal or social paradise, though he came to have a moderate amount of wealth and could have made a considerable attempt at it. Instead, he distinctively waited to receive a kind of home that would be far better than anything he could get through his own means.

Here I found the core of Abram's spirituality, this is how

his beliefs and life were essentially different from those around him. It was the first major discovery in my search for the heart of gold. Abram paid a price for his difference, and though he came to terms with it, his descendants did not always do so. I understood that the way Abram's children were going to meet the challenge of his unique spirituality would form a large part of the epic story.

4. *The covenant*

Abram received his promise as part of a special "covenant" between him and the High Power, whom he called *El Elyon* (meaning "Highest Power," or traditionally "God Most High"). It was when the covenant was made that this childless man trustingly took up the name of *Abraham,* which means "father of many nations." Since so much of our own recent world history implies the question "Which one of Abraham's sons is the rightful heir of the homeland in the Middle East?" I wanted to have another look at the wording of the covenant as we have it in the oldest documents, before moving on with the story.

First and foremost, the covenant was about how important Abraham himself would become: "I will bless you and make your name great, and you shall be a blessing... and in you all the families of the earth shall be blessed." In the successive versions of the covenant that are given in the Genesis document, the close friendship between Abraham and his God is highlighted. The main issue, therefore, was not land but rather a relationship with the High Power through which protection and blessing was given: "Do not be afraid, Abram, I (myself) am your shield, your exceedingly great reward."

Genesis repeatedly states that there will be "many nations" coming from Abraham through his descendants, and this aspect of the promise relates to both Ishmael and Isaac. Not only Abraham but also Hagar, Ishmael's mother, specifically and significantly received the divine promise that "I will multiply your descendants exceedingly so that they will be too numerous to count."

Nevertheless, there was a distinction made. When the covenant was formally "cut," meaning that it was established through a ritual, Abraham that day received a prediction about the land:

> Know for a certainty that your descendants will be strangers in a country that is not theirs and will serve them, and these will afflict (your descendants) four hundred years ... but in the fourth generation they shall return here (to Canaan)... To your descendants I have given this land...

Islamic and Jewish traditions each acknowledge that both of the first two sons of Abraham (for he had more later on) are children with a promise. On the basis of the covenant's wording, however, it has been clear that it was Isaac's offspring who went to a country not their own and came back to Canaan four centuries later, while Ishmael and his progeny stayed in the southern deserts. So the key question as far as the modern conflict is concerned is not about the original promise of land — it is generally acknowledged that Isaac was supposed to get it.

That clarity, however, won't solve the problem of land ownership if the covenant promise contained a condition, a requirement that had to be followed in order for the promise to stand. And indeed, there was just such a caveat, a warning and stipulation about the intended blessing. In Abraham's family, all the males had to be circumcised, "and the uncircumcised male child... shall be cut off from his people, for he has broken the covenant." Circumcision, like a sacrifice, was held to be an indispensable symbol of a man's obedience to the High Power and a token payment for lack of obedience in himself and his family.

So, the promised land was not fully assured to all of Isaac's descendants. The promise, after all, was part of the two-way characteristic of the covenant: the pledge of a gift, and the recipient's response to the pledge. There remains then an important issue: did Isaac's descendants forfeit their covenantal right to the land, and would such a forfeiture be permanent?

This is not an idle question to be pondered by some ivory-tower theologian. Though our book is not the place to debate this sensitive and controversial issue, such matters were the very ones that occupied most of the ancients whose documents we are examining. Many times, the people of old would be thinking, "Since I belong to God, why do I experience so much trouble? Why should my blessings not be more secure?" The ancients considered such matters to be quite important.

5. Abraham's consistency

At the time that Abraham graciously conceded the better pastures to his relative Lot, the record shows that he heard God say to him, "Look around you to the north, south, east and west, for this land that you see I will give to you and to your descendants for all ages... Arise, walk through the length and breadth of the land because I will give it to you." In response, Abraham went south toward the settlement of *Hebron*, moving through the southern part of the promised land, but did nothing to lay claim to it. Nor did he build himself houses and barns as he prospered materially in his occupation, but remained living in tents.

Some time thereafter, he came to the aid of the king of Sodom and other rulers in that region after these were beaten by a combined force of Mesopotamian armies. Possibly drunk with triumph and going separate ways with loot, the victorious Mesopotamians turned out to be easy prey. They were put to flight by a force of three hundred and eighty men that Abraham had quickly managed to assemble. His motive in this was not conquest but only the safe return of his nephew Lot and his family, who had been taken captive.

When the grateful king of Sodom offered Abraham a large treasure as reward for the rescue, he refused it, saying, "I have sworn by the Highest Power who owns the heavens and Earth that I will take nothing, lest you say that you made Abraham rich." I was impressed with Abraham's surprising decision not to accept payment. By walking away from the reward, he was able to maintain his independence and freedom of action, declaring that his greater obligation was to his God.

Neither did his success in battle give him the idea to start enforcing ownership of the promised land. Abraham dismissed the fighters and just went back to his daily life, to the tents and the undeeded pastures. Nevertheless, though he remained a temporary resident, he had no qualms about owning just a little bit of property for practical reasons. When servants of *Abimelech*, the Palestinian (or Philistine) ruler, seized a well that Abraham had dug, its builder complained to him. Abimelech then made a formal agreement to yield possession of the well at the nominal sale price of seven lambs.

And so, Abraham meekly and diplomatically purchased his own well from the Palestinian ruler. Not only that, it was located in the very land pledged to him as his own. He did not take a fierce and uncompromising stand on his rights but was willing to negotiate. Near the well, a tree was planted to commemorate the humble purchase and the place was thereafter called *Beer-Sheba*, Well-of-the-Seven. Abraham then lived in peace among the Palestinians "many days."

The only tract of land recorded as having been obtained by this sojourner was a large field that contained trees and a cave, though he bought it only for a graveyard for his family. Some say it was located near Hebron, others that is was in Jebus which later became Jerusalem. Medieval sources and more recent scholars have generally favored the Hebron site, Christian Crusaders built a church over a burial cave in that location, and a Muslim mosque rose over the same spot. In any case, the field was owned by Abraham as a cemetery and not as a place of residence, business, or a seat of power.

It is remarkable that this man, despite having a promise of land and being active in society, was so consistent in his aim to avoid entanglement with the worldly places and ventures that others were striving after and claiming. As we said before, Abraham was nothing short of exceptional.

6. The lives of the sons

Emotionally caught up in the rivalry in her home, Sarah one day had enough of it and evicted her servant Hagar from the family, along with Ishmael. The latter two went to live somewhere to the south, likely at a small oasis where Hagar had been spiritually encouraged before the birth of her son, though according to Muhammad's revelation Abraham escorted them all the way into Arabia. Ishmael eventually married a woman from his mother's native land of Egypt and continued to live apart from his father. However, it was near enough so that when Abraham died, Ishmael very soon heard the news and came up. Together with Isaac, he buried his father in the cave of the purchased field.

After the funeral, Ishmael returned to his own home with no uniquely-promised land to claim as an inheritance, but according to Genesis, his growing family gradually spread out over a wide desert area ranging from Shur (just east of Egypt) to Havilah (just to the west of Mesopotamia). Meanwhile, Isaac still wandered around the district of Beer-Sheba in southern Palestine. Neither of the two sons tried in any way to possess the promised land of Canaan during their days on Earth, and to that extent at least, their lives honored the memory of their extraordinary father.

Chapter Three
Finding important themes

1. In children's hands

Up to the present point in my search, I had not been disappointed. As the story began to develop, it seemed that the epic was not religious advice literature at all. It was an account of human life and understanding, with worldwide and ages-long implications. To me this was important stuff, and I remained hopeful that the documents would unfold a spirituality as opposed to a religion. I would have to let the documents speak for themselves and just hope that a heart of gold would reveal itself.

The story, at any rate, remained interesting. One of Isaac's cousins, the young woman *Rebekah,* was brought to Palestine from Charan to be married to him. Then Isaac lived with her the rest of his life, being a hardworking, straightforward, God-honoring man like his father and walking in his father's ways. Some of the son's stories seem to have been confused with some of those of his memorable father, and indeed Isaac was his father's faithful but smaller version, a man who successfully lived in Abraham's shadow. The human side of the covenant was safe in the son's sincere hands.

It was an entirely different matter when the next generation came along. Isaac and Rebekah had a set of self-willed twins named *Esau* and *Jacob,* both very unlikely heirs of the covenant promises. Esau was much like his father in personality and preferences except that he cared almost nothing for the covenant of Abraham. He probably never really understood it. He loved physical thrills, not the mindful things of the spirit, and spent much of his time away hunting. When Esau left home, he married two Hittite women whose hearts were as cool to the covenant as his own was. When he discovered how displeased

Isaac felt about this, Esau tried in his uncomplicated way to make amends by taking a third wife, this time from their own clan, one of the granddaughters of his uncle Ishmael.

It was no better with his brother Jacob, who turned out to be a swindler of the first order. Jacob cheated his twin out of the birthright that was his brother's due and even conspired with his mother to steal his father's death-bed blessing away from Esau. Naturally, he didn't get this bad all at once but must have gradually strengthened his hand through trickery to make up for his inferior physical skills compared with those of his sibling. Jacob was not one to openly face an opponent in a fair fight.

Even when he saw in a dream a ladder extend into the heavens with angels ascending and descending on it and the God of his fathers speaking words of comfort to him from above, it did not actually seem like much of a blessing to him. Though he named the place where he had the dream *Beth-El* (House-of-God), he felt awed and afraid, rather than thrilled or inspired. Instead of responding to the occasion by turning his life over to God, he offered the High Power a sincere but shrewd offer: "If you bless me enough, I will give you one-tenth of all my possessions and will let you be my God!" It was the cautiously calculated offer of an insecure man, not a model for prayer.

After Beth-El, Jacob traveled on, fleeing a furious Esau, and arrived at Charan in Syria. There he ended up working quite a long time for his uncle *Laban*, a two-faced man who took advantage of him but then paid for it dearly by the success of Jacob's enterprising tricks. In the end, Laban's sons watched the wealth of their own inheritance disappear into Jacob's pockets and were as furious about this as Laban himself was.

Now the way Jacob figured it, his new wealth was all part of God keeping the divine side of the bargain at Beth-El. His tendency to always cheat a little kept him from seeing what the fuss in the family was about, but his wives Rachel and Leah, both daughters of Laban, urged him to leave as soon as possible.

So he stole away without letting his uncle know, taking a large amount of livestock and worldly possessions with him.

2. *A turning point*

Jacob plodded on with many sheep, goats, servants and their families, two wives and many portable possessions. At a stop along the way, he had another Beth-El type of experience in which he saw angels (this time a whole army of them), and once more he felt fear rather than inspiration. He was also afraid at the prospect of meeting a still angry Esau, who was rumored to be coming up from the south with a force of four hundred men. In order not to be wiped out completely, Jacob divided his people and herds into two companies, sending them out in different directions while he stayed behind alone to think matters out carefully and pray fervently for deliverance.

There by his campfire, far into the night, he was suddenly met by an unknown and barely-seen man who did not answer his hailing. Was it a bandit, or one of Esau's men, or possibly even the stronger brother himself?

For once in his life, Jacob took on the challenge without trickery or weapon and engaged the intruder in hand-to-hand combat. They fought for a long time without either of them scoring an obvious win. Just when day was breaking and their faces were becoming clear, the stranger put Jacob's hip out of joint as they wrestled. Now having the advantage, the opponent surprisingly asked Jacob to let him go. But he said, "I won't let you go unless you bless me!" The man then asked for his name and when Jacob had answered, he said, "No longer Jacob but *Isra-El* is now your name, because you wrestled with God and man and have won."

The new name meant something like "Winner-with-God," and Jacob interpreted the whole incident as meaning that he had struggled for God's blessing in a desperate situation and despite his own sins had gotten divine approval. When he was alone again, he called the place *Peni-El* (Face-of-God), for he said, "I saw God face-to-face and my life is spared."

All kinds of theological and historical questions have been raised about the incident at Peni-El, but I very much wanted to stay with the story itself. I allowed myself to make two straightforward observations. The first was that both Abraham and Jacob experienced their God in tactile, human terms — that is, they both spoke with what certainly appeared to be a man or someone much like a man. No ponderings seem to have bothered them about how the High Power could be in the heavens as a purely spiritual being while at the same moment on Earth as a man. And secondly, the strange incident altered Jacob in a way that was hinted at by his change of name. He had fairly fought his opponent to a stand-still and no longer had to prove himself. There was no need to cheat now or steal the blessings, no need to take a different road from that of his grandfather Abraham. He had achieved a new inner identity, a stronger sense of self. He had at last become, like his grandfather, a friend of God rather than a bargainer, and the covenant was now renewed with him.

Then, contrary to Jacob's earlier fears, when Esau arrived he proved to be a generous and forgiving man who determined to make the family reunion a happy occasion. There was first a good amount of feasting with his much-relieved sibling, and afterward the big man departed for his own adopted home south of the Dead Sea. With Esau gone, Jacob gathered up his two companies of people and livestock. He could have followed his brother south to where the old stomping grounds of Hebron and Beer-Sheba lay, but he chose a new path. Jacob turned fatefully to the west.

3. Life in the world around

Jacob's story and other tales of the goings-on in the families of Abraham's offspring were not at that time of any interest to the nations and societies in that part of the world. The day would come when all that would change forever but for now there were other challenges to face. Far to the east of Palestine and Canaan, the family's ancestral home of Sumer had seen a restoration of ancient Semite rule as a king called Sargon of Akkad spread his sovereignty over the land. This notable ruler, of the same general ethnic race as Abraham and various Middle East nations, had passed on by the time Jacob lived. A few centuries later the great Hammurabi would come to unite Sargon's territory with his own, thereby establishing the Old Babylonian Empire that covered most of the ancient land between the two great Iraqi rivers, the Tigris and Euphrates.

North of Palestine, a large and growing tribe known as the Hittites (Esau's wives, for example) had spread their influence from what is now Turkey down to the borders of Canaan. And to the southwest lay the significant civilization of Egypt, in existence almost as long as Sumer had been, and whose Old Kingdom pyramids were indeed quite old by Jacob's time. In fact, the younger Middle Kingdom was then living out its last days as well.

All over that part of the globe, people were seeking to hold onto land or to conquer it, to live among old glorious monuments and rulers or to set up new ones of their own in hope of fame and immortality. There was an ongoing battle of empires, while at the local level people jostled for space to graze their cattle or moved around to escape robbers and the troublesome presence of war-lords. In general, people at all levels, for their justification or for protection, called on powers of nature in the guise of their particular collections of gods and goddesses.

In that kind of a world, the challenge for Abraham's family lay in distinguishing their own unique understanding of the High Power they called El or Eloh, and to keep their attachment to this God distinct from the way El was worshipped by the Semitic tribes around them. Particularly, the household needed to practice circumcision and sacrifice for their own distinctive reasons. Such rituals were not unique to Abraham's family but special covenantal significance was associated with them and that meaning was absent in other clans and tribes.

Cultural separation from others would either play a major role in the lives of Abraham's descendants or it would be quite forgotten along with the reason for the separation. And if not remembered, the descendants would begin to live according to the cultures of those around them, setting aside their ancestor's unique spirituality and covenant promise.

4. An aborted settlement

A tragic and historically influential event was about to take place for the clan of Israel. It was an appalling incident that would affect the lives, territory and religion of Israelites for centuries to come. After leaving the family reunion of his brother Esau, Jacob came to Shechem, a small fortified town in the mountainous region west of the Jordan River, situated by a landmark called "The Oak (or Terebinth) of Moreh." It was a memorable place, for here Abraham had ended his journey from Charan to Canaan, and now Jacob also decided to rest here, having traveled back from Charan by way of Peni-El. Unlike his grandfather, however, Jacob hoped to settle down here, so he bought a large tract of land near the town walls where he set up an ownership marker in the form of an altar to God. It must have been a comforting thought to finally have his very own home in a protected location — and yet it was not to be.

One day, when Jacob's lovely daughter Dinah was visiting the women of the place, the son of the local ruler took her aside and forced himself on her. Despite the sexual aggression, the man remained infatuated with her and urged his father to get Dinah for him as a wife. The father did just that, but Jacob's sons entered the conversation, tactically withholding their fierce anger about the mistreatment of their sister. Though prostitution and other sexual indulgences were casually practiced among them, the incident with Dinah had greatly offended the family's pride and solidarity: someone had dared to insult the Israel clan, and that (in a tribal society) was cause enough for serious retaliation.

No law had yet been given to the Israelites, so everyone took care of his own form of justice. There was no equitable "eye for an eye" in vogue here but rather any fierce revenge, no matter how extreme. Deceitfully, Jacob's sons made a promise to support the proposed marital union if the men of Shechem would agree to be circumcised as all the men with their father were. The people in the town, discussing it among themselves, found circumcision an acceptable price to pay for access to all of Jacob's herds, money, and women.

Therefore, on an appointed day, the whole adult male population of Shechem submitted themselves to circumcision. The mass operation must have been done with a great deal of ceremony and good humor as the city took a step toward a wealthier and brighter future. Later, when Shechem's men could hardly move because of soreness in their privates, *Simeon* and *Levi,* two of Jacob's sons, went among the population with sword in hand and murdered them all. Then the two plundered the town, taking its gold and silver, its women and its children.

Jacob, however, was badly shaken by the news and terribly displeased with the enraged violence of his two sons. He quickly made preparations to leave the area before the city's neighbors could take their revenge. Family members purified themselves, along with those of the Shechem women who agreed to go with them for protection, by giving up all superstitious trinkets and "teraphim" (small statuettes of gods). They buried the amulets near the city and departed in haste for the notable location of Beth-El, where Jacob made sure to impress the story of the covenant on his whole company.

So began another period of unhappy wanderings for Jacob and his family. Canaanite tribes nearby did not attack out of fear of what had been done at Shechem but neither was the family welcome. While brother Esau was establishing himself to the south and his prospering sons were preparing to become chiefs of large households, Jacob/Israel and his people pitched tents wherever they found some pasture and felt safe enough to stay for a short while.

Years later when he lay on his deathbed, Jacob still chafed from his sons' violence and the price the whole family had paid for it. In the bitter memory of the massacre, he would withhold his final blessing from Simeon and Levi, but would give their brother Judah leadership of the extended family until the covenant's promises were to come true.

Not long after Jacob's forced retreat from Shechem, the fortified town was again inhabited by Canaanites and it came to play an important role in the epic in future years. Today, the Palestinian city of Nablus is located on the site of this ancient town, and there the error of the sons of Israel is kept in memory.

5. *The agony and the wisdom*

It was in this time period that the story of *Job*, a tale that possibly originated among Esau's people, seems to have been adopted into the repertoire of Jacob's family. Jacob had now personally experienced the harsh truth that bad things do happen to good people. It was not long after his hopeful change of outlook at Peni-El that he had come to endure the consequences of the Shechem Massacre, a tragedy not of his making. He may have prayed, "Why now, when I was just starting to get my life together?"

The question of why the righteous suffer is the focus of the life of Job, who was a just and good man serving others, but he lost his own family, possessions, and health. His heartbreaking story developed into a long poem that replied to the question by setting his difficult experiences on a higher plane, within the context of larger issues of which people on Earth are scarcely aware. In Job's case, suffering involved the hostile interference of the ancient Rival. Through the long agony he suffered, Job learned to move beyond the kind of simplistic thinking that Jacob had used in proposing a deal with God at Beth-El (the "I'll serve you if you give me what I want" type of faith).

In the story, it was the bargaining mentality that the Rival thought would be an opportunity to destroy Job. "Does Job serve you for nothing?" the Adversary said as it taunted God. Then it proposed that if the man was seriously harmed, he would surely curse God. In the ordeal that was permitted following this discussion, Job's faith and character were painfully put to the test, but he survived and matured with God's own intervention. Goodness and faith proved stronger than tragedy and evil. Job was then even able to intercede for judgmental "friends" of his who had tried to force naive advice on him in the midst of his suffering. In the end, Job recovered fully and was doubly blessed for the rest of his life.

It was an instructive long poem, well-suited to be of help to Jacob and (as we will soon see) to his favorite son Joseph. In response to life's unfairness it counseled neither emotional reaction nor moralizing, but instead the quieter wisdom of viewing harmful experiences in a larger frame. In a refreshing departure from advice literature, the poem, while exposing the misguided instruction often given to those who suffer, doesn't imply that the alternative is always straightforward and easy. Though advocating inner wisdom, the book of Job contains a long passage that expresses how hard it can be for anyone to find wisdom, especially in the midst of distress and pain. A few brief excerpts:

> Man puts his hand to the flint,
> overturning mountains by the roots
> as among the rocks he cuts tunnels
> to see valuable stones.
> He even dams up flowing waters
> to bring to light what hides beneath,
> but – where shall wisdom be found,
> and the place of understanding?
>
> Man knows not its worth, no,
> that is not found in the land of the living...
> It is hid from the eyes of all the living,
> even from birds in the sky.
> Also Death and Destruction say,
> "We only heard of it with our ears."
>
> God alone understands its way,

he knows where it is.
...He confirmed the place, explored it,
and then said to man:
"Clearly, respect for God is wisdom,
and turning from evil — that is understanding."

6. *The Egypt years*

The Shechem Massacre forced Jacob's family to live apart from people around them, a difficult experience that nevertheless helped to preserve the covenant and the outlook on life that Abraham had earlier taken up voluntarily. On Shechem's dark cloud this was the silver lining, a ray of hope that influenced Jacob's favorite son Joseph, the famous boy with the coat of many colors. Joseph's remarkable life has become known around the world, even being re-enacted in a popular rock opera of our time. And what a satisfying story it is.

In a rage of jealousy, Joseph's older brothers sold him to Ishmaelites of Midian, who in turn pawned him off to a wealthy Egyptian named *Potiphar.* The possible ruler of Egypt at this time was Ni-ma'at-re Amen-emhat III in the 16th century BC. This pharaoh had a high official called Podipa-re (probably the biblical Potiphar), warden of the Memphis state prison, whose wife's name was Nofret.

Nofret made sexual advances on Joseph and it was by rejecting these that he paid dearly for his integrity. Joseph spent nine long years in prison before being summoned by Pharaoh to interpret some prophetic dreams. The prisoner was then made *Vizier,* chief advisor to the pharaoh who believed Joseph's prediction of seven years of plenty and seven years of famine. Pharaoh also offered Joseph a wife from the Egyptian nobility and put him in charge of securing adequate food for the whole population.

When the forecasted great famine arrived and lasted, other people from the east came to Egypt hoping to find pasture and to buy grain. Among them were Jacob's other sons. After repeatedly testing their present minds and attitudes, the Vizier

Joseph, overcome with emotion, revealed his identity to his brothers and called for his father to come to Egypt along with all his family, workers, and possessions. An aging Jacob arrived in the Nile's delta-land of Goshen and died there peacefully seventeen years later. Joseph took Egyptian guards and professional mourners with him and went to bury his father in the cave that Abraham had bought for the family. He then returned to Egypt and lived in honored retirement in the delta city of Avaris, where archeologists say Joseph's empty tomb has been found.

Such is the nutshell version of a fascinating life. After Joseph's death, local rulers in Goshen seized power and started a period of great instability in the land of Egypt. Foreigners in the country began to be exploited. The ancient historian Artapanus of Alexandria identified "Khenophres" as being a pharaoh who oppressed the inhabitants of Goshen. Indeed, it was a ruler of the similar Egyptian name of "Khanefer-re" who managed to reunite the traditional land of Egypt along the Nile with the delta of Goshen and to start on major construction plans. For this the pharaoh needed many slaves, and so we have the beginning of the renowned story of Israel in slavery, of Moses, of the Exodus out of Egypt, and of the attempt to give Abraham's family a land of their own at long last.

I sat back after all this re-discovery and rested. The journey was going well enough and I felt that I was avoiding two traps. I was not reading the documents as if they were Sunday School lessons while at the same time not brushing them away as pre-scientific myths. A number of main themes seemed to be revealing themselves through the stories so far. There was a long way to go still, but I remembered that sometimes a journey itself is the main thing, and not so much the destination. I would press on, hopefully to a renewal of Abraham's spirituality, or else to a better understanding of what went wrong. At the very least, I could take in the epic as pretty good literature.

Chapter Four
Qualms and instructions

1. The long run

In the middle of some of my research, it suddenly dawned on me that maybe one of the reasons there are so many versions of Abrahamic religion is the simple fact that the span of the epic is many centuries long. The story's lengthy development has brought about many efforts to highlight one particular "chapter" of it in order to reduce the whole thing to something more easily grasped and palatable. I suppose most of these efforts were well-meant but they were basically mistaken attempts at removing the *epic* quality of the story. We would all like to grasp things quickly and be able to boil everything down to our level of understanding, but sometimes it just cannot be done so easily.

A patience-testing experience strengthens us in the long run if we stay with it, and this is deeply reflected in the epic as an important aspect of its message. We can appreciate the protracted story better if we're able to relate a bit to its pains-taking lengthy development. For those who have known extended times of painful waiting in their own lives, the epic's length confirms reality. It seems to say that here is an understanding which is anything but flighty.

As we've seen, until the birth of Moses none of Abraham's descendants were established in the promised land, and no such settlement was to take place even in Moses' lifetime — which was about *six centuries* after the promise was made. One wonders how many Israelites in Goshen still believed in the covenant, and what inner resources were being strengthened or damaged by this state of having so long a pledge without the fulfillment.

At least they, as slaves and "temporary residents," had no chance to try building their ideal home-on-earth by dominating or mistreating their fellowman, though some might say that's not much of a silver lining. It may not have felt like much of that to the slaves, but the Israelites had a great deal to learn and to unlearn. Without inner changes, if they did inherit the promised land they would quickly become like other nations, grasping their territory and wealth and never having enough, becoming willing to do almost anything, however devious and misguided, to get more worldly security.

Such, after all, was Canaan or this is what it had become during the years that Jacob's people were away in Goshen of Egypt. Though people there officially worshipped God as El, their actual daily lives and interests revolved around the male and female deities called *Baal* and *Asherah*, thought to be part of El's court. By and large, the inhabitants had succumbed to the view that their fertility and prosperity depended on sexual feelings in these gods. In the centuries after Jacob, as historians and archeologists have discovered, Canaanite religion developed increasingly bizarre and repugnant rituals in which sexual acts were committed by priests and worshippers. Even the sacrifice of little children was practiced in various locations as offerings of the fruit of fertility.

These tragically-deluded abominations showed that Canaanite society had somehow become mired and was sinking downward in a spiral of depravity. How then could the Israelites, if they ever returned to Canaan, possibly withstand the extreme moral slide they would find there and avoid being sucked under by destructive practices and beliefs? It was a vital question, one on which the eventual success of the covenant appeared to depend.

2. Years of preparation

The one really hopeful sign was the superb quality of the man who aimed to lead Israel out of Egypt. Moses was one of many little Hebrew boys cleverly snatched from destruction by Egyptian midwives who chose to disobey the evil execution order of an obsessive pharaoh who feared his slaves. After being rescued from death and quietly adopted into a branch of the royal household, Moses grew into a young nobleman with a heart to see justice done for his oppressed relatives. But after he killed an Egyptian for beating an Israelite, he fled into the wilderness to escape the reach of Pharaoh's swift retribution.

In the well-known story, Moses found his way to a distantly-related clan in the Sinai peninsula and settled down. There he married the daughter of a Midianite, one of Ishmael's descendants (or possibly, because the name is the same, the family may have been of the line of Abraham's sixth son, Midian, and therefore another distant relative). Now living among these nomads who worshipped the same God as his kin in Goshen did, Moses the "Prince-of-Egypt" had become a refugee, the exact kind of "pilgrim and stranger" for whom Abraham's covenant was intended. Like Abraham, Moses let go of country and possessions, along with social advantages. In the desert, half-way between Egypt and the covenant's promised land, he lived out years of delay and waiting, learning that even the promise was not as important as the restoration of trust between the people and their High Power.

After many years in Midian of Sinai, Moses was one day confronted by the strange sight of an apparently-burning bush that was strangely unharmed by the glowing fire, and there he first heard the voice of God. Unlike Abraham and Jacob, he experienced the divine not in the familiar form of a man but in the awesome sight of an unnatural occurrence. From the day of this visual wonder on Mount Horeb in Sinai to his death decades later on Mount Nebo at the edge of the promised land, Moses' task was to help instill the fear of God in the Israelites and to institute a demanding type of worship.

Was this then the occasion that Abraham's spirituality was forever side-tracked in favor of rules-oriented, strict religion with all its scrutiny and judgments? I knew that many people have made such an argument but I found that to be a little too hasty. It is true that the severity of what Moses presented in the desert is something few modern people, apart from religious fundamentalists, can appreciate. However, I discovered in the sources a clear reason for the strictness: "You must guard all my laws and judgments and perform them so that the land where I am bringing you to live will not vomit you out." The purpose of the strict rules was to warn Israel against participating in the hideous wrongs of Canaan lest they forfeit their right to the promised land. There was no point liberating Israel from Egypt just so that it could get lost or destroyed in Canaan's severely polluted society. Something had to keep them on a more beneficial path.

The promise of getting Canaan was not free after all. It would be fulfilled at the price and obligation of moral and ethical separation from the culture to which they were going. In other words, Israel had to have a chance of becoming as unique in outlook and life as Abraham had been when he lived in Canaan. The picture here was not all about harsh religious authority. It was more a matter of a good parent or teacher keeping the kids in line and hoping to protect them from bad friends.

This is much the same sense that I got from the account of Moses seeing a bush burning but not burning up. There he heard a voice say to him, "I am the Eloh of Abraham, the Eloh of Isaac, and the Eloh of Jacob." That sentence connected to the past, but next Moses was instructed to use the name *Yahweh* when he spoke to speak the people: "Say to the children of Israel, 'Yahweh, the Eloh of your fathers...'" The name Yahweh translates as "I am who I am" and at the very least meant that Moses and his people were not to tailor their ideas about God to suit their wishes or to pattern him into their own image or in the image of other people's notions of deity. The name's meaning seemed to say, "God is who he knows himself to be, the same yesterday, today, and forever." Down through the years, the Yahweh name was a reminder to Israel of a God who did not turn back on his promises and who had given them the serious responsibility of being unique in the very disturbing land of Canaan.

3. Preparing to leave

The slaves in Goshen, who were known by their dialect of the Syrian language as *Hebrews,* did not welcome Moses as their leader upon his return from Midian of Sinai in the company of his brother *Aaron.* No, like most oppressed people anywhere, they were more interested in immediate relief than in any long-term project of eventual freedom. The pharaoh was even less impressed and marked the occasion of Moses' return by ordering the Hebrew slaves to gather their own straw, which until now had been provided to them to use in the process of making bricks. Israelites connected the two events and directed their anger more at Moses for showing up than at their Egyptian task-masters for their harshness.

In the familiar story of the Bible and of movie director Cecil B. DeMille, dreadful plagues came to afflict Egypt at this time when Pharaoh dismissed Moses as a spokesman for Israel. Though the massive plagues called into question the power of Egypt's ruling class and their gods, they had an equally shifting effect on the minds of the Hebrews. Coming by Moses' predictions, these calamities served as much to convince the Israelites to follow him as to persuade Pharaoh to let the people go.

Later, just before they left Egypt, Israel observed the first *Pass-over* feast. They put lamb's blood on their doorposts and ate the lamb's meat while standing up in traveling clothes, ready to depart. Along with the meat, they consumed the fast-food of unleavened bread and bitter herbs, and hastily followed all of Moses' careful instructions about the observance. That very night, the firstborn Egyptian males died mysteriously along with all the firstborn of the livestock, but death *passed over* the homes where lamb's blood had been placed.

Pharaoh then finally gave the word for the Hebrews to leave the country, and being ready, they hurried to get out. The Egyptians gave them whatever they needed, so long as they would leave and never come back (which of course was the whole idea on Moses' part). At his instruction, the Pass-over observance remained an important commemoration for Israel. They continued to keep the feast for many years and it is still celebrated annually in our own times by Jews the world over.

The route of the great Exodus is well-described in the document of the same name, with place names at every turn. After the stirring trek through the Sea of Reeds and the drowning of the cavalry of the changeable Pharaoh, the Israelites moved south through the Sinai peninsula. They weren't used to being free and to take daily responsibility for themselves. For three long months of bone-wearying, dusty travel, they complained and rebelled, talked of going back, and were moreover attacked by an opportunistic band of Amalekites, a warlike desert tribe. Liberation wasn't much fun after all.

At long last, the fatigued and dissatisfied company of thousands arrived in Midian of Sinai and set up their camp just below the mountain where Moses had seen the non-burning bush. The place was bleakly remote, a long way from Egypt and just as far from the borders of the promised land. Mount Horeb looked like a set of gigantic rock pillars leaning over against each other, foreboding and somber, bearing little vegetation. It was the kind of location that reflected the starkest realities of life, inspiring awe or fear, silence or an urge to escape, but this is where the covenant would be renewed with the entire nation.

4. *Lessons in being the distinct society*

On the third day of the camp, Moses brought the people to the foot of the mountain and warned them to go no further. While everyone watched, a thick, smoky cloud descended onto the peak, the earth trembled, and a lengthy, loud blast like that of a giant ram's horn trumpet was heard. The leader bravely climbed high up the slope in order to converse with Yahweh. When at last he returned, Moses spoke to the people in a loud voice all the words of the Ten Commandments.

> I am Yahweh your God who brought you out of the land of Egypt, out of the house of bondage. You shall have no other gods before me...

The people heard the words but sent Moses back, urging

him to be their mediator with this terrifying deity. Being scared stiff and not wanting to stay so close to the mountain, they would much rather that Moses relay God's messages to them in the camp, at a slightly safer distance.

The Hebrews' request for distance was granted and before long there were many more commandments given through their leader. Israel now had the beginnings of a whole body of law, as well as quite precise instructions for making a Tent of Meeting (traditionally called the Tabernacle), for building a sacred golden chest called the Ark of the Covenant, and for all things pertaining to priesthood and sacrifices, down to small details. Through these laws and commandments Israel would learn how to be "God's unique people" — that is, they would know how to distinguish themselves in every way from the nations to which they were going.

At the end of one of Moses' sessions on the mountain, he descended the slope with stone tablets on which some of the laws were written. Meantime, however, people down below had intimidated his brother Aaron to gather gold from everyone and with it to make a golden calf, just like some of the representations of Baal and other gods of Canaan and Egypt. Then Aaron, completely against the notion of Israel's uniqueness, stood beside the calf he had made and said, "Israel, this is your God who brought you out of the land of Egypt!" The people then brought food offerings, "sat down to eat and drink, and rose up to play." Though they hadn't yet even seen Canaan, they were pretty well starting to get the hang of things there, enmeshing their religion with sexual or suggestive acts.

Still back on the heights, Moses pleaded with God to restrain his wrath at the people's wrong-headedness, but when he reached the foot of the mountain and saw their forms of worship up close, his own anger boiled over. He smashed the stone tablets in his hands and went down into the camp to thoroughly destroy the golden calf. There was clearly a whole lot of work to do before the covenant people would be anything like Abraham.

5. Ownership of the land

This was not only an old account about a nation distant in time. In some ways, it has been the story of people in general, and of western civilization in particular, with many familiar themes. Over the course of four decades of living in the Sinai, Israel gradually learned, but didn't eagerly follow, the growing body of law. Part of the reason the law grew so large was that much of it was "case law," pointing out what was right and wrong for a variety of specific cases. Certain laws would say, "If this kind of situation occurs, then here is what you must do or not do." In order to explain how to live according to the spiritual and ethical principles of the commandments, more and more particular examples and clarifications were given as time went on and as actual cases were heard and decided on. A knowledge of the law became more important but also more difficult to achieve.

Most of those who came out with Moses in the Exodus never really became committed to adopting the moral and ritual standards that the law required. Having experienced long years of bondage in Egypt, they were just not inclined to submit to a new master and new rules. Being grateful for liberation didn't always translate into wanting to be responsible and distinctive citizens of the planet. The bitter memory of having been forced to bow their heads to slave-drivers in the past now made them "a stiff-necked people" who were intent on being their very own masters.

Even if some Israelites became serious about keeping the commandments, the law was not as spiritually beneficial as the priests said it was. If we follow the suggestion in Job's story, we can imagine that the shadowy Rival, unsuccessful at stopping the spread of human influence on the planet, would find a way to spoil it for them. It would not take the Rival long to figure out that it had been handed a mighty new tool. After Sinai, the people of Yahweh could no longer plead ignorance of the divine will as an excuse for any wrong-doing, and they were therefore quite guilty. Here is an aspect of the religious law that is often overlooked: it makes sin even more sinful than it already is.

Since the law now spelled out in some detail on stone and parchment what Israel's obligations were to the High Power, to fellowman and to nature, an Adversary might say to God, "Look how these people of yours are consciously sinning because they know the commandments. Therefore, according to this law you must curse them with punishment or death." Intending to advance a destructive end, a Rival might even learn to quote the holy books against God and the people in order to hinder humans from inheriting the Earth. In any case, that's how it would have looked from the ancient perspective of the book of Job. The law could be a curse as well as a blessing.

6. *The crucial admonition*

Since many Israelites, despite the law, continued doing only what was right in their own eyes, one possible motivation for greater self-discipline might be the need to band together to fight an enemy. This is something they would certainly have to do as they got closer to the promised land. The older generation, however, had no interest in warfare. It was only after most of those who could remember the Exodus had died of old age that Moses was able to take Israel out of Sinai and into territories along the eastern shores of the Dead Sea, approaching Canaan from the southeast.

Before the venerable leader himself died, he had the entire law repeated to the whole nation, making it clear that ownership of Canaan was going to be conditional on living by the commandments. If the people became law-abiding citizens in the new country to which they going, they could hold title forever and be blessed. The firm warning, however, was that if they became law-breakers, they would forfeit their right and be cursed. That curse would include being attacked by surrounding nations and eventually being removed from the land in order to serve foreigners once again as slaves.

This admonition might have appeared exceptionally harsh to some, and indeed Moses presented Yahweh as a deity more to be feared than loved, "a jealous God" who would tolerate no rival. But though Israel didn't fully grasp it, they were to accept the new identity of being God's chosen people, a nation with privileges and serious responsibilities like those of royalty. They were going to be a country of stewards, a kingdom without a king, as well as a nation of priests in the metaphorical sense of living by the sacred law which they, as well as the professional priests, could know.

By way of contrast, Canaanites had a very different view of themselves. According to what the incoming Hebrews were soon to discover, a Canaanite did not trust his own knowledge and decisions but received daily advice from "witchcraft, a fortune-teller, an interpreter of omens, a sorcerer, a conjurer, a medium, a spiritist, or one who calls up the dead." There were various reasons why these practices were forbidden to Israelites. Not only would such reliance on the views of others hinder their opportunity to grow in their own special identity, but the Canaanite practices were especially associated with their moral decline. If Israel got swept up into them, the decline would be their lot as well.

Life, however, is often decided by the weakness of human hearts and the poorness of human memories ("...some things that should not have been forgotten were lost"). As the mobile tribes of Israel stood at the borders of Canaan, their excitement and amazement pushed specific warnings far away. They had not yet really seen Canaanite culture nor could they at this threshold of conquest grasp the possibility of their own decline and the loss of the land they were about to enter.

Chapter Five
"We want a king"

1. Warnings

If the ancient epic was only a story about a certain people and how their God gave them their promised land, we could expect this present chapter to be the last, as it tells of Israel entering Canaan, taking it, and beginning life as a nation with its own borders. Or if it was a handbook of religious teaching and rules concerning a particular faith, we could also soon bring the matter to a close, now that the Hebrews had Moses and the law. But if the epic is a story of how the life and outlook of Abraham either spread to the world or was distorted in the attempt, how the heart of gold either grew to become a spiritual hope for many or became lost to us all, then we realize that we still have some way to go in the overall story.

It struck me as quite peculiar that in this epic Moses, the great law-giver and religious architect, did not die a hero's death but was prevented from entering the promised land on account of his own imperfection. What an odd twist that was in the life of Israel's national founder and prophet, who was said to have been "very meek, more than anyone on earth." In the end, he was only allowed to see the new land from a distance on top of a mountain. And why?

Here was a question of some importance, as I discovered. The reason Moses was kept from entering the Canaan was that one day, in a rage against his people's obstinate behavior, he had misrepresented Yahweh's character to them. This was a very serious matter because Israel depended on him to be God's spokesman and to tell them what God was like. Still, to most of us it seems a severe punishment for him to be kept out of the land that he had lived to introduce to his people. Yet that is what the law was about: to convince people of the spiritual problem of broken life, but not to provide a lasting solution or a definite way out. And so, the great leader disappeared mysteriously one day up the mountain, his body never being found, and Israel being unable to honor him by bringing his remains into Canaan.

Moses had understood the matter better than most people either then or now. Though he learned to control his angry outbursts, he had not been very positive about his nation, and he thought the years' long dream of seeing a kingless "holy kingdom" might die with him. In his final address to the new nation, the old man looked into the future and saw that though Israel would be given success against the Canaanites, an appalling era awaited them after that victory. He predicted that his nation would switch their allegiance to the religion of Canaan, leave the sacred law, break the covenant with Yahweh and forfeit his favor.

Still, like a true leader, Moses blessed the people and paid a verbal tribute to his own Levite clan who were the designated religious professionals, though they wouldn't be allowed a tribal territory in Canaan on account of the Shechem Massacre. The offspring would pay for the sins of the fathers. In this regard, though Moses spoke well of the other clans of Israel, he omitted in silence the tribe of Simeon, Levi's partner in violence.

After the unexpected disappearance of this great prophet and statesman, his successor *Joshua* led the wandering tribes over the Jordan River into the promised land where, in the words of the American spiritual, he "fit the battle of Jericho and the walls came a-tumblin' down." Less famous are the many battles that followed this initial victory, but the often-held opinion that the Canaanites were largely wiped out in a genocide goes much too far. Israel's stated objective was to "drive out the inhabitants of the land." They were often agreeable that any inhabitant who cooperated with this aim could be allowed to leave peaceably, or in some cases even be permitted to stay among them.

By the time of Joshua's death, when Israel was largely in control of the promised land, there were at least twenty-one districts in which Canaanites held onto their property. While many inhabitants of these areas paid tribute money for the privilege of staying, they were generally left in peace. Also left alone was most of Palestine, which traditionally included five coastal cities (in the now famous "Gaza Strip") as well as adjoining territory to the south.

Such clemency was not without danger. In his own leave-taking at the end of his life, Joshua later repeated the gist of the final words of Moses, warning the people against their tendency to forsake the covenant and switch to foreign ways. He gathered the leaders together at historical Shechem as a reminder of the possibility of losing the promised inheritance. To emphasize the importance of the place, Joshua buried there the mummified body of Joseph which had been carried all the way from Egypt, and there he set up a large memorial stone as a witness against Israel if they should ever forsake their covenant God. This is probably the very same rock that is still standing upright today in the ruins of Shechem in the Palestinian city of Nablus!

2. The downward spiral

The situation after Joshua died was fragile. There was no king in Israel and national loyalty was supposed to be given to Yahweh and the law. No central figure arose or was appointed to unite the tribes, who were now beginning to work the land of their more-or-less independent settlements. Without a king or capital city, each tribe and clan carried on as they themselves saw fit.

For the next two centuries, a repeating pattern evolved in which Israel gradually accustomed itself to Canaanite culture, even becoming attached to the local gods and their fertility rites. In due time the Canaanites, seeing that the feared Israelites were actually much like themselves, lost their awe of the invaders and began making inroads, sometimes winning back certain districts and towns, and taking their revenge. Eventually, some Israelites would return to calling on Yahweh, begging God to remember the covenant and rescue them from oppression. A leader would then arise among them, lead a counter-assault, restore order and the law of Moses, and become an advisor and judge of the people until his or her death.

The nation always stayed decentralized throughout these events, each of Israel's tribes living more-or-less on their own within a loose union. Since there was never a direct successor to leadership, during the in-between years when no national judge existed, Israel again drifted into following Canaanite ways, the Canaanites once more became bold to attack, the people again cried out to Israel's God for help, and a new leader became the national judge. And so the cycle continued.

The overall trend, however, was decidedly downwards as the judges grew less effective in turning people back to the covenant. Israelites sank low in spiritual confusion and moral decay. Once, in a fit of anger, they even massacred their own tribe of Benjamin, nearly exterminating it. When the new nation was at a very low point in its cycle and night was at its blackest, a ray of light appeared one last time in the person of a new judge.

An intelligent man called *Samuel*, trained in priestly duties, began to act as national leader, urging people to put away their idols and turn solely to Yahweh for deliverance from the Palestinians. He called Israel together for a day of prayer and fasting, but when they came, Palestine took this opportunity to send a formidable fighting force against the large prayer assembly. Unexpectedly, a very severe thunder storm formed quickly in the path of the attackers, triggering chaos among them. This providential event allowed the Hebrews to launch a counter-assault and to drive the enemy back a far distance.

Samuel memorialized that hopeful victory by setting up a large rock that he called *Eben-Ezer*, "Stone-of-(God's)-help." The name Ebenezer has since been given to many places and people, sometimes out of tradition but also to reflect a hope that the place or person would be secure by the power of faith (or in the case of Charles Dickens' Ebenezer Scrooge, first fallen by the power of money, then restored). After the battle of Eben-Ezer, Palestinians and Israelites remained at peace for the rest of Samuel's life.

3. The renewal of the kingdom

When Samuel was old and in failing health, he made his two sons administrators of his priesthood and judgeship, but these younger men did not have his spirit and used their positions of authority for dishonest personal gain. It was starting to become painfully obvious that law and order were, by themselves, powerless to build Israel into a holy nation. The Hebrews now realized that a way had to be found to retain the benefits of properly strong moral leadership beyond the rise and death a national judge, but how that could be done was a difficult question. The elders of all the clans then gathered in Samuel's town to tell him their own solution to the problem: "Make us a king to judge us, like all the other nations."

The national judge was stung by the sudden proposal to replace him. He took time to pray about it and heard God tell him not to take it personally, that it was not a rejection of his judgeship but of God's rule over the chosen people. But Yahweh also appeared to be agreeing to the proposal for his own purposes, and accordingly when Samuel returned to the elders, he stopped short of a rejection of what they proposed. Instead, he lectured them about the negative side of a king's autocratic powers. If they wanted a government that was "like all the other nations," they would have to put up with compulsory labor, expropriation of the most productive fields, taxes in the form of tithes, and the transfer of their income to the king's relatives and favorites. In the end they would likely regret their choice. But the elders would not change their minds and so eventually Samuel agreed to appoint for them a king.

"What a dumb mistake," I thought, but then recalled that the notion of Israel as a kingdom was not new. Way back in the Sinai desert, it had already been said, "You shall be to me a kingdom of priests and a holy nation." The concept at that time was a theocracy in which God ruled and all the people were priests in the figurative sense that they were each other's equals, to help one another live distinct, holy lives. There was no real king, though it could be said that Yahweh ruled and all Israel was his queen or royal family.

Consistent with this peculiar version of a kingdom was Samuel's instruction to place on the throne an unassuming and hard-working person of limited ambition, someone to be taken from the weakest Israelite tribe. In other words, this man had to be more like a steward of the nation than a royal owner — a significant distinction. So Samuel was sent a man called *Saul,* a tall fellow from one of the lowest families of the little clan of Benjamin. Upon the head of this man of humble origins the judge poured scented oil as the symbol of God's special authorization, and later a more formal coronation took place in the presence of representatives of the whole nation. The unpretentious Saul (who even hid himself to avoid the honor) initially made no great impression on people but in the words of Samuel, the time had come to "renew the kingdom" — as if it had already existed before.

4. An unrenewable king

The early years of Saul's reign were promising as he proved that he had some quality, though with more time he also showed himself capable of impulsive stupidity. A few years into his reign, having won some battles and feeling more secure, Saul sent his son Jonathan with Israelite troops to attack a Palestinian stronghold where captured Hebrew weapons were stored. Palestine had forbidden Israel to replace captured armaments with new ones, and Saul's idea was to get many of the weapons back. In the attack, the Palestinian defenders were slaughtered, but their countrymen then reacted by coming against Israel with the largest force they had ever assembled, comprising thousands of chariots and cavalry in addition to an even greater number of foot soldiers. Too late Saul realized his weak position, particularly because he still had a significant shortage of weapons.

When Israel's soldiers saw the great Palestinian host advancing, they trembled and ran for cover. "Let the Levites be gathered to me," Saul nervously ordered, "or anyone who can quickly prepare sacrifices." The king hoped that such offerings would assure him of success against the superior force but he was not permitted to make the sacrifice himself, being neither Levite nor priest. Urgently, he sent for Samuel to come and consecrate it. But the former judge, probably disagreeing with this war, delayed his arrival.

Noticing this unexplained postponement, even men around the king began to defect. Then as he watched his force shrink by the hour during Samuel's baffling absence, Saul took it on himself to make the hope-giving burnt offerings by which he intended to stem the tide of desertion and rally the troops. This action broke an important principle in Israel that there be a clear distinction between acts of worship and rulership, or as we might say today, "separation between church and state" (even Moses, with all his divine contact and prophetic writings, had not been allowed to take over the role of priest or worship leader).

However, the king pressed on and as soon as he had made the sacrifices, Israel's old judge finally showed up. When Samuel saw what Saul had done, he vowed angrily and loudly that the kingship would be taken from him. Samuel then departed as abruptly as he had come.

The day was saved when *Jonathan*, the crown prince, made a daring commando raid on a Palestinian garrison, killing about twenty men and causing widespread confusion in the camp by the element of surprise. Israel found opportunity to attack swiftly and thereby achieved a significant victory that moved the conflict further away. But Saul got into one of his moods and said, "Cursed be the man who eats food before evening when I have taken vengeance on my enemies!" So his fighters had to keep on battling for hours without replenishing their strength.

When Jonathan returned from the raid later in the day, not having heard his father's order, he ate some wild honey. The famished Israelite troops saw it and rushed on any animals they could find, eating them raw with the blood — something strictly forbidden by the laws of Moses. When the king heard what his son had done, he was enraged and prepared to kill him for disobeying the order. But the people looked on Jonathan as a hero and vowed to prevent the execution.

Though Saul managed to win additional battles, his personal fortunes plummeted. After the king made more foolish decisions and showed increased disregard of Yahweh, Samuel secretly anointed another man to the headship of the nation and by so doing gave birth to a splinter group. The king eventually became aware of this growing opposition but was frustrated in trying to stop it. In time, the sovereignty was taken away from him and his house. Israel's initial experiment with a monarchy had turned very sour and, even more ominously, had begun to split the loyalties of the people.

5. *A man for the hour*

This was a critical time. From being too negative and too focused on immediate needs during the wilderness years, Israel had become too quick to accommodate while the damaging influence of Canaanite depravity was still potent. Then the new nation wavered much in its cyclic and always temporary return to the covenant, and their superior legal constitution proved incapable of inspiring them toward noble lives or to put an effective check on their bent for lawlessness. Now with the reign of the hapless Saul, any further setback could affect the nation's future for a very long time.

It was at this crucial moment that Samuel had anointed a young man named *David,* the same who became known the world over as the youthful hero of the David-and-Goliath incident. The young man grew into a warm-hearted and likeable leader of a widening group of dissidents. Most of his active support came from Israel's southern region where his own tribe of Judah was in the majority, but David also had other allies. Among these was the king of the neighboring nation of Moab, along with the independent-minded Achish, ruler of the Palestinian city-state of Gath, and even Jonathan, the presumed heir to the throne.

Despite his opposition, David always made sure he spoke

respectfully of the king in front of his men. He actually denied himself a few excellent opportunities to kill Saul: once when the king was sleeping in a nearby camp, and once when Saul went to relieve himself in a cave where the band of renegades was hiding. On both occasions the young leader spared his enemy's life and let him leave without his dignity but otherwise unharmed.

Like Abraham, David had received (by his anointing) a life of great promise, and just like Abraham, he declined to lay claim to it until its time. Though the need to be a fighter had been thrust upon him, he was a man of high principle and a lover of the covenant law who could be ethical to a fault. No wonder that Samuel was told God had found himself a man after his own heart.

Most of us would have liked David. Good looking, he was also open and human. Though personally courageous in action, he often composed songs about his fears. When he had fled from Saul to a cave, he wrote:

> My soul is among lions,
> I lie in the midst of people fired up,
> whose teeth are spears and arrows
> and whose tongues are sharp swords.

When Saul sent assassins to a house where he was staying, David sang a prayer:

> Though I did them no wrong they run over,
> ready to kill.
> Wake to my help, and see this!

And on another occasion, while in deep distress, he said:

> Won't someone give me wings like a dove
> so I can fly away and be at rest?
> How I want to flee far away
> and stay a while in the desert!

Through his songs, David released his feelings but also encouraged himself by remembering the times God had helped him. One fateful day, when it was reported that his royal enemy Saul and the crown prince Jonathan had died in battle, he expressed genuine sorrow. To the surprise of many, he wrote for the occasion a lament that he taught Israel to sing. It is called "The Song of the Bow" and contains a short refrain which is still famous today: "How the mighty have fallen!"

David's band of outlaws now met with representatives from his tribe of Judah in Hebron, where the tombs of the covenant fathers were, and there they anointed him king. Eventually, all Israel agreed to the kingship of "the Son of Jesse" (as David was also known), and when the last Canaanite hilltop stronghold of Jerusalem was finally captured, it became the new capital city. Now the singer-songwriter-soldier and king took up residence on the city's hill, called Mount Zion.

This significant event marked the start of Israel's "golden age." When the Hebrews then and later spoke of "the kingdom of God," what they meant was their own country under the stewardship of David and his sons.

6. *Marks of the Golden Age*

Despite his principles, sensitivities and attractive humanity, David was still basically a warrior — strong of body, strategically crafty, quick of mind, willing to kill when necessary, and fearfully respected by opponents. He fought many kings and extended his sovereignty considerably. Under his rule, Israel became the major power between Egypt to the southwest and Syria to the northeast. Yet it was clear that he did not want to personally dominate Israelite society as an idol or demagogue. In fact, he saw himself as a servant of a greater king, namely of the High Power.

David had the understanding that God was "Yahweh of the hosts" — in other words, a great commander who fought rivals and destructive forces. He sang many psalms to this war-like God and was able to compose such lines as:

> Blessed be Yahweh, my rock,
> who trains my hands for war, my fingers for battle…
> Yahweh said to my Lord, "Sit at my right hand
> until I make your enemies your footstool."

These were not just "religious" sentiments. They expressed both the king's personal feelings and his political philosophy. As a lord of men, David truly believed that he did not own the kingdom. As lord of the land he served under another lord, the High Power who coached his victories and kept a rein on the king's powers and prerogatives. As if trying to remind himself of that outlook, he brought the Ark of the Covenant to Jerusalem and made plans to have it housed in a great new temple.

However, a man called *Nathan,* a prophet known to the king, after first agreeing to the plan changed his mind. Returning to the royal court, Nathan told David that God was not in favor of the project. Instead, Yahweh promised, "I will build *you* a house," by ensuring the line and dynasty of David's own clan. Apparently, the half-legal institution of kingship was not beyond redemption and redefining, and it might be useful until something better could come along.

Was this then, I thought, the pattern for specifically spiritual matters as well? Was it advisable to look at one's own spirituality and at society's religions through long lenses, allowing far less rigidity and more adaptation to changing times than is often the case? And are people's desires to please God all too often against God's will? I told myself to stick with the story for now, to stay with the flow rather than start making conclusions that might be too analytical or simply premature. I reminded myself again that these stories were not written as Sunday School lessons or as sermon material. The epic was unfolding as it should, and I had to read on just to absorb and enjoy.

A Kingdom for the Heart

A timely retelling of an ancient epic

The epic falters

Chapter Six
A house divided

1. Domestic breakdown

> Now in the days of your youth
> call to mind your Creator,
> while days of evil have not yet come,
> when the years do not yet strike you
> so that you say, "I have no pleasure in them."

An author simply looking for a good story might have been tempted to end it right here with the triumph of the Golden Age, but the epic kept going a lot longer. The above excerpt in effect reminds us "to number our days" because life does wind down. That is as applicable to a nation and civilization as it is to a person. After Saul, Israel at last grew into a successful kingdom, even one superior to their immediate neighbors, but in that Golden Age seeds of division and destruction were sown, so that "days of evil" were bound to come.

Before the era of the monarchy, wrongdoing was often attributed to the people in general, but with the arrival of Saul the focus of error was right at the seat of power, and this view of the social problem was continued by the ancient writers of the nation's history. The main fault was with the king. Likewise with David, who rarely had to contend with a serious challenge to the throne from outside his house, but he was weaker within the nation, and this was at least partly his own doing.

One of his sons went to a pretty step-sister and asked her to lie with him. When she refused, he forced her. The girl's brother, *Absolom* (Avsholom), soon found out and he hated the rapist. When David heard of it he was very angry but took no action. Perhaps he did not dare punish a son for something similar to what he himself was guilty of, for David had committed adultery with the beautiful Bathsheba and had made sure that her husband, a Hittite and a good man fighting for Israel, was killed in battle.

Not waiting for the king to come to a more just frame of mind, Absolom plotted to avenge his sister. He threw a party to which he invited all young members of the royal household, and planned it as an opportunity to kill the rapist. When the guilty prince was merry with wine, Absolom's servants brutally struck him down in the sight of the guests, and the avenging brother fled to a neighboring kingdom to escape the consequence of taking matters into his own hands.

Over the course of time, Absolom was pardoned and allowed to return, but he was not yet finished with his plans. This firebrand was good-looking, ambitious, an effective public speaker, and he continued to bear a strong grudge against his father for not having brought the rapist to justice himself. After returning to Israel, the prince began a campaign to win the hearts of people, getting to know them and luring them with thoughts of how much better he would make their lives if he ruled.

When he thought he had garnered enough support, Absolom went to Hebron (in the manner of his father) to have himself proclaimed king. On his side were those who had formerly favored the house of Saul, together with many of the younger generation. He was also supported by people who bore various private grudges and those who disliked David's frequent wars, together with the people who were scandalized by his adultery. All these now joined the conspiracy so that it grew very strong.

In response, David made haste to flee east to the Jordan River. Urging his faithful priests to stay behind in Jerusalem to be his eyes and ears, he traveled with members and servants of his large household, in addition to the core of his army. There was also a contingent of loyal Palestinians from the city of Gath where he had once stayed in exile, for these people had also become refugees when the political tide had turned in their homeland. Along the road of the royal retreat, a man with foolish rage followed them, throwing stones and cursing the king for his earlier victory over the house of Saul. Any of the soldiers could have killed the man but the king forbade it and bore the humiliation. David remembered that he should subject himself to the High Power even when much provoked by circumstances.

The fleeing company crossed the Jordan River and came to the place where Jacob, on returning from Charan, had envisioned an army of angels. In that inspiring and now fortified location, David regrouped and made his military strategy, sending his best fighters back to challenge Absolom's forces.

In the ensuing battle, Absolom got his prized long and wavy hair tangled in the branches of a tree, and against the king's strict orders, the insurgent was killed by David's own general. Then, while the rebel force was being cut to ribbons, the son of Jesse mourned the loss of his own son with many tears and loud crying which the town could hear. "O Absolom! My son, my son! Would that I had died in your place!" The moment of victory began to feel like a day of shame as the people across the Jordan walked through the streets troubled and in silence because of their leader's personal agony and public grief.

Before long, the king was brought back to Jerusalem and the throne, from where he publicly forgave the angry man who had cursed him on the road. Though this act of mercy may have persuaded some to bury their issues with the king, David never regained warm support from Israel as a whole. A manifesto was soon being sung in various districts of the land by the more openly rebellious among the people who were refusing to serve:

> There is no share for us in David,
> no inheritance for us in the son of Jesse.
> Israel! Each man back to his tent!
> Now see to your own house, David!

2. A conflicting heritage

Major troubles did not leave the kingdom after Absolom's nearly successful coup, for David's prestige had been irreparably damaged. Unfortunately, he didn't help matters any. Overriding the cautionary objection of his own general, the king insisted on taking a census of Israelite men who were able to be used for military service. A couple of the ancient documents indicate that this unpopular act was a major blunder and they lay the blame for it in confusing ways, placing the responsibility at the feet of David but also blaming the people themselves, God, and even the Rival.

In any case, the man who had been known both for his might and humility, limped to his death at the age of seventy, having reigned seven-and-a-half years in Hebron and thirty-three more in Jerusalem. Time would dim the memory of his faults, and when members of the royal family later kept the throne despite doing evil in the land, some said that God was remembering David the Good and the promise to reserve the rulership for his heirs.

The king was remembered as a solid friend of the God of the fathers, setting a strong example of loyalty to the greater King. David always seemed to be aware that in spite of his preoccupation with politics and war, the key promise and hope of the covenant was not the land or royal glory but rather the faithfulness and mercy of the High Power. "My goodness is nothing apart from you," he sang to God in one of his many compositions, and his renowned "Twenty-third Psalm" catalogues the deep benefits of the relationship: "Yahweh is my shepherd, I have no lack ... he restores my soul and leads me in the right paths..."

On the other side of the balance, the reign of the son of Jesse invited the serious problems of his later years. The strong support and closeness he enjoyed with his own kin in Judah aroused jealousy in the rest of the country. The envy ran particularly deep in the territory of Ephraim where there was a considerable religious history, including a traditional site of Yahweh worship at the town of Shiloh. These Ephraimites and their neighbors were none too happy about being eclipsed by an increasing focus on Jerusalem. And besides the growing centralization of worship, David adopted much of the political form of other monarchies in that part of the world, having acquired the trappings of success as he built a large palace for himself and for his increasing number of wives and concubines.

All these changes undoubtedly added to the feeling of many Israelites that they were becoming strangers in their own land, not because it was owned by others but because they were more and more disconnected from their nation's seat of power. This feeling of alienation was later to erupt openly again with serious and permanent consequences.

3. Splendors of peace

Jedidiah, the son of David and his famous mistress and wife Bathsheba, ascended the throne under the name of Shlomo, king "of peace" (sh'lom), whom the world knows as *Solomon*. The new ruler benefited from the regional peace that his father had won with much blood, and he learned to administer it superbly, becoming a master of state diplomacy. With increased trade, many years of good agriculture, fewer military expenses and a treasury full of tribute payments, Solomon embarked on major engineering and construction projects. Adding to the size of Jerusalem by leveling the adjacent hills, he had workers erect a huge platform of stone blocks whereon he built a house for Yahweh.

Solomon's renown during his own lifetime has persisted. Even in our own day, the saying "wise as Solomon" is still widely used, and he certainly proved to be wise in a variety of ways. First, as we said, he knew how to administer the peace and keep it. Secondly, he shrewdly increased his treasury by acquiring the best fields and vineyards, leasing them out for a part of the yield to feed his large household. Moreover, king Solomon's mines and industrial sites were well-known, and he traded heavily with Egypt and other nations.

In a remarkable move, Solomon sent ships south to Africa

to obtain precious metals, ivory, and other material. Even more surprising, as an alternative to the southern route going through the Red Sea, some of Solomon's ships joined the Phoenician fleet heading westward through the Mediterranean and beyond Gibraltar to find additional lands where goods from tropical Africa could be obtained. The thought behind this expedition was only a step away from the idea of sailing around the whole African continent, a feat that would have been truly historical, though there is no indication that it happened at this time.

Thirdly, Solomon became a great advisor to his people, holding audience to answer their difficult questions and to help them solve their more trying disputes. Many of the wise proverbs attributed to him were perhaps first spoken in these sessions of mediation and counseling. And lastly, Solomon was a dedicated scholar who specialized in biology, bringing specimens to Jerusalem for study: apes, monkeys, exotic birds and many plants.

Though it has become fashionable in some modern circles to diminish this man as being just a minor ruler of an unimportant, dusty land, there is much to suggest that the more favorable ancient portrait of him is essentially correct. His fame spread far and wide even in his own lifetime, as shown by the long journey made by the Queen of Sheba in Southern Arabia specifically to see his wonders. On the surface, the glorious reign of Solomon was the height of Israel's existence as a nation and many still see it as being such, but underneath all the splendid accomplishments the foundations were already beginning to shake.

4. The musical mirror

Quite apart from the breadth of his knowledge and wisdom, Solomon's power and success bred corruption. Contrary to the laws of Moses, he loved many women, extending his harem of wives and concubines to hundreds. Many of these were merely formal, political and diplomatic marriages, but for the more important of his foreign wives he built lavish homes and shrines where they could worship the gods of their own lands and where he, by obligation of state and bed, worshipped at their side.

His many building projects, in addition to a mushrooming national administration, required much forced labor from non-Hebrews living among them, as well as taxes and occasional work duties from all Israelites. People paid heavily for the king's glorification of the land by his mega-projects. It was a nation in which the rich were getting richer and the poor poorer, but for all his justly famous knowledge and wisdom, Solomon seemed blind to these dangerous developments. It's so much harder to be wise for oneself.

As the king grew old, dissatisfaction came more into the open from both Israelite and foreign sources. There is no documented evidence that he was ever faced with rebuke from a prophet such as Nathan, but there has survived a critical literary work called the "Song of Songs" (also known as "The Song of Solomon").

This musical composition is a series of poems depicting the struggle of an attractive, darker-skinned young woman from northern Israel who is brought to the royal courts. Torn away from her shepherd lover in order to be trained in Jerusalem for possible addition to the king's harem, the girl from the fields hears the laughter of her fairer urban colleagues in the beauty school who cannot understand why she is not thrilled at having this opportunity. Solomon shows up and woos her with sensual but splendidly formal poetry while the shepherd can only wait anxiously behind the latticed windows of the harem school.

In the climax of the Song, just when the king seems to have won the girl over, she makes up her mind to turn down the opportunity that the daughters of Jerusalem crave, and returns north to be with her rustic lover.

> O, I think of his left hand under my head
> and his right hand embracing me.
> Listen to me, daughters of Jerusalem,
> hear what I say, women waiting for love.

> Do not contrive what you hope for love
> and put on no show to arouse.
> Do not stir up nor awaken love
> till it comes to you of its own.

The superbly-crafted Song of Songs reflected with exceptional skill the nation's relationship to Yahweh, an attachment of faith that had become far too identified with the cause of the capital city and the clever devices of the court. The advice to the "daughters of Jerusalem" is not just to avoid relying on sexual techniques instead of a genuine relationship; on a deeper level, the Song wanted them to think again about being too easily impressed with outward appearances in regard to the spiritual aspect of life.

The Song of Songs also reflected some of the jealousy and dissatisfaction of Ephraim and the rest of Israel's rural northern region which increasingly opposed the reign of the son of David. One of these opponents was a man called *Jereboam*, who rebelled against Solomon's policy of building Jerusalem into a large central city. For this, the Ephraimite was threatened with arrest and punishment, but he managed to make his escape and lived for a number of years in Egypt as a political refugee.

5. Divorce at Shechem

When Solomon died in old age, Jereboam quickly came home to see how he might help bring about change. Together with other leaders in Israel he now called on *Rehoboam*, the son of Solomon designated to be king, to meet with them at Shechem before the coronation. It is interesting that they chose neither Jerusalem nor Hebron, but rather set the stage in Shechem, that old symbol of warning to Israel and of opposition to Levite influence.

Being young and still lacking insight, Rehoboam came unprepared for the challenge set before him by the people gathered in Ephraimite territory. Before any coronation, they first wanted to know if he would extend or lighten his father's unpopular policies of centralization, high duties, taxation, and the endless number of work gangs for large construction projects. The crown prince could have prevented open rebellion had he not at this time listened to wrong advice, but he decided to react harshly to the assembly. They were shocked to hear him say in crude language that he would abuse them more than Solomon ever did ("My little member is thicker than my father's loins"). Infuriated by this degrading answer, the people cut short their audience with the prince and turned into the streets.

Soon the crowd was singing the rebellious old manifesto of David's time ("There is no share for us in David..."), a protest song with a long life, like the modern west's "Solidarity Forever" or "We Shall Overcome." When Rehoboam again responded recklessly by sending to them the reviled minister of tribute (that is, of revenue and forced labor), the exasperated protestors surrounded the man and stoned him to death.

The prince quickly returned to Jerusalem for his own safety while the elders remaining in Shechem established a new dynasty, headed by Jereboam. This man of Ephraim garnered the support of most of the country (officially he got ten out of twelve tribes, though the real numbers are more ambiguous), leaving Judah and the house of David largely by themselves. The Golden Age had ended in angry division.

Jereboam made the emblematic town of Shechem his hub of operations, honoring the tomb of Joseph, the worthy ancestor of the large northern tribes of Ephraim and Manasseh. The break-away ruler aggravated the divorce from Jerusalem by setting up decentralized places of worship at the upper and lower extremities of his new realm. Then, getting caught up in his own revolution, Jereboam gave the radical order that a statue of a golden calf be placed at each worship location to stand in for Yahweh, the deity that was too closely associated with Jerusalem. Though some Yahweh worshippers remained in the northern kingdom for many years, the official religion there was well on the way to becoming something quite different from that of the Abrahamic heritage. From the covenant point of view, these developments were an absolute disaster.

The northern kingdom kept the name of Israel while the southern remnant was called Judah. This division was never healed and the sense of being sibling nations in a common home-land diminished over time. The northern defection from the ancient covenant became permanent as each successor to Jereboam confirmed the court's opposition to the ways of Yahweh, leaving only the Judah-ites (the Jews) to take up the challenge of remaining faithful to the covenant and the law.

I was beginning to see with more clarity some of the problems with Abrahamic religion. The division of Israel, far from being a footnote of ethnic history, came eventually to shed some light and have an effect on the spirituality of many people in many nations. Co-incidentally in the present stage of my research, a number of prophets who spoke about the problems now started to come along. These voices of challenge and change are the subject of our next chapter.

Chapter Seven
Prostitutes and prophets

1. A weariness

Here was the mouth of the cave, the entry point to a dark labyrinth where the gold might be found or forever lost — that was the feeling I had at the opening of the era of the prophets. The deep mystery of the heart of gold would either start to penetrate the darkness or the value of the search would have to be re-examined. The reason, I suppose, for this feeling was simple: any half-insightful observer in Israel after the time of the kingdom's division could justly have said that the covenant way wasn't working very well. It had offered little protection against appalling behavior, nor did it seem to stand up well against competing dreams and beliefs. It all sounded vaguely contemporary and modern to me. In any case, if Abraham's legacy was not to disappear altogether, there had to be a gleam of light soon.

Many persons of that day were thinking that there must be a better approach for getting what they wanted out of life. The times they were a-changing, and the covenant way was proving to be little of a match for the sexual excitement and material promise of the fertility religions. In the midst of many rapid social changes and personal stresses, the lure of linking spiritual hope to both prostitution and prosperity, as the Canaanites had done, was such a titillating temptation that many in Israel could not resist looking further into it. Some Canaanite religious rites openly made use of temple prostitutes, their erotic "worship" somehow promising wealth for all from the gods. Perhaps Hebrew men could go there for a bit of pleasure, telling their wives they were going out to do their religious duty and make a patriotic contribution to the health of the economy.

There was nothing particularly wrong with wanting to prosper but that desire also made it easy to forget old "Father Abraham" and his unique way of living life. Nor was there anything in the religion of Israel, either in its creation stories or in its law, to suggest that sexuality itself was wrong. The issue was more about the way in which prosperity and sexuality were being linked together, and about how gratitude for both was being shifted from Yahweh to "the Baals," the supernatural lords of Canaan. It was that "link" and "shift" that soon brought voices of protest to the fore.

2. The troubler

It was a time when several men in both Israel and Judah began to speak out against the trends that they saw. One of these persons stood out among all the rest, his reputation being second only to that of Moses. That man was *Elijah* of the northern kingdom. He lived mostly by himself but was still passionately involved in the life of his country, and his personal habit of wearing rough clothing woven of camel hair became a uniform and symbol of office to many later spokesmen who were inspired by him.

Elijah is best known for his unbending opposition to the royal couple of *Ahab* and *Jezebel*, who were proud promoters of the fertility religion of Baal. Ahab called the fierce prophet "the troubler of Israel" and Jezebel persecuted all those who worshipped Yahweh, murdering so many of them that Elijah mistakenly thought he was the last one alive of their number. The royal pair particularly hated him for the severe drought that he had prayed and called for. It happened exactly according to his prayers and the long dry spell only came to an end three years later with a spectacular contest on Mount Carmel involving Elijah and the promoters of the fertility gods Baal and Asherah.

In the spiritual competition on top of the mountain, those who were favored by the royals shouted out to their deities, cut themselves with knives and danced furiously in an unsuccessful attempt to bring heavenly fire down to burn the bull lying on their altar. Then Elijah, having poked fun at them and their sleeping or vacationing gods, heavily soaked his own altar with water and prayed, "Yahweh, answer me so that these people may know that you are the Power and that you turn their hearts back to you again." A huge flash of fire struck the altar and consumed the sacrifice. While the audience was stunned by the amazing spectacle, Elijah quickly had the fertility priests and prophets executed. Later that day the rains finally returned to Samaria, in driving torrents.

Jezebel flew into a rage at the news of these events, vowing to have Elijah arrested and killed within a day. Hearing of her threat, he hurried to flee into Judah, leaving his employed helper with the Jews while continuing on by himself into the southern desert. He ended his flight weeks later at Mount Horeb, where the law had been given to Moses long ago. Despite his previous supernatural feats and protection from violent death, Elijah was only a man and he now sought to hide in a cave where he could nurse his deep fatigue, anxiety, and depression.

After sleeping a long time, he stepped out on this mountain of Moses (*Jebel Musa* in Arabic) where there had once been smoke, thunder, and quaking at the presence of Yahweh. Perhaps he hoped for the same sort of drama to lift him out of his agony. Indeed, that day he did experience a very strong wind, a quaking of the ground, and even a fire caused by either of these events. Yet the skilled man of God did not sense a special divine presence in any of these natural phenomena.

But after these things came a strange quiet, the slender sound of silence like a still, small voice. Then Elijah knew that God was near. The noise of confusion in his head disappeared, his emotions stabilized, and he knew he was on the right track again. Wrapping his mantle over his face, he waited at the cave's entrance. Suddenly, a clear voice spoke with him and he received new instructions for his work.

Such was the strange life of one of Israel's greatest prophets.

3. The crazy man and his message

Within these disorderly times, there was a man of God who deliberately chose as his wife a prostitute well-known in his community. The wedding was very public and set tongues wagging for a good many weeks. Some people were scandalized, others said he was trying to make an honest woman out of her, and most just laughed that he must have married his favorite hooker. The couple tried to ignore all the gossip and just get on with their lives. Her name was *Gomer,* his was *Hosea.*

About the time that the rumors and merriment finally died down, a boy was born to the couple. That event again got the public's attention and renewed some of the talk. Then a year later came a daughter, and afterwards another son. Each time that Hosea announced to the public his newborn child, he also gave them a prophecy. The first son was a sign that the northern kingdom would reach a violent end. Hoping for a boy with a better name and message but getting a girl as his second child, Hosea said that God would no longer have mercy on Israel. The birth of another son provided no encouragement either, at least not publicly, for Hosea declared that his name would be Lo-ammi, which means "Not-my-people," and he said Israel was no longer Yahweh's own chosen nation.

At each occasion, the peculiar man, his scandalous wife and their children, caused a buzz in the community as people spread the news and Hosea's words. The prophet in this way received a hearing for his messages even though their content was negative and unpopular. His main theme was that the real scandal lay with the northern kingdom of Israel, which had committed spiritual adultery and was not at all sorry. Originally belonging to Yahweh, the kingdom (also called *Samaria*) had "gone whoring" with the Baals for extra sexual pleasure and economic prosperity.

People could respond as they liked. Did they think Hosea was a crazy fool? It was only a reflection of their reality, he told them. "The prophet among you is a fool, the spiritual man is insane, because your sin and hostility is great." Did they dislike his children and the names or meanings given to them? They were only signs that God did not much like the children of Israel because "they are the children of harlotry." *Spiritual* harlotry is what was meant here, though sexual excesses had also become common in the northern kingdom.

Hosea felt his message personally. Prostitution and adultery touched off pain in his own heart, for it seems Gomer was not faithful and she was eventually separated from him. He married again, a woman who is not named but who also had committed adultery before. Once more, Hosea felt he could not escape God's intent to speak through his life, for he said that just as his new bride would no longer be in circulation, neither will Israel be seen anymore. The kingdom will end and only after a long time will their children return to the land to seek Yahweh their God once again.

In case it had not been entirely clear before, it was slowly becoming much more plain. This was all about a relationship. The land was important too, but without the relationship the land would be lost. Prosperity and sex were important as well, but without the relationship they were nothing more than games and prostitution that would be destructive in the end. The clarity of the picture presented by poor "Hosea the fool" grabbed people's attention, though he paid a heavy price to get this message out to those who needed to hear it.

4. The bigger picture

> Fallen she has, not to rise again.
> On her land the virgin Israel lies forsaken
> and no one raises her up.

So sang the poet-farmer *Amos* of the northern kingdom as he undertook one of the most difficult tasks a prophet had to perform: to speak meaningful sense to people in a time of doom. First, a prophet had to acknowledge the troubled questions of his own mind as the world around him began to fall apart, and then he had to speak to people who would blame God for the tragedy they saw coming or were already experiencing.

The message, given in ways unique to each prophet, always carried a common theme. The significant point was that God was neither absent nor helpless nor uncaring, but the universe was unfolding as it should, according to the necessity of greater things than people normally consider. The best response to upheavals was always to turn back to God from the errors of business-as-usual and from the uncaring ways in which people treated each other.

The prophet *Joel*, also from the northern kingdom of Israel/ Samaria, wrote that even an expression of regret over the wrongs was not the most important point:

> Tear your heart and not your clothes,
> return to Yahweh your God,
> for gracious and merciful is he,
> slow to anger and of great kindness,
> and he recoils from doing harm.

Joel's understanding was that some battles would not go well and some lives would be lost, so that personal hopes and dreams would have to take account of the bigger picture. In the greater scheme of things, it was important not just to follow feelings but rather to accept the divine work in which mankind had a share, a future and a purpose.

Habakkuk, a man who agonizingly questioned God about the violence and environmental collapse of his time, ended his complaint with this challenge to himself and all others:

> Though the fig tree does not bud
>   and there is no fruit on the vines,
> though the effort of the olive fails
>   and the fields produce no food,
> though sheep have not returned to the fold
>   and there is no herd in the stalls –
> yet I will celebrate Yahweh,
> rejoicing in the God of my rescue.

5. Twilight comes

Finally the end approached for Israel. The kings of Samaria, having been opponents of Yahweh without exception, reigning as they pleased and opposing the prophets who challenged them, pressed forward head-on in a downward spiral as the northern kingdom forfeited its covenantal claim to the promised land.

In the year 722 BC, Shalmaneser, king of Assyria, got wind of political double dealings by Hoshea king of Israel, who was officially his vassal but was conspiring with Egypt against him. Assyrian armies came down and began the harsh process of removing the entire nation of Samaria, resettling most of the Israelites in dispersed territories far to the north. The next Assyrian king, Sargon II, imported various foreigners to take over the now empty Samaritan territory. The evicted "Lost Tribes of Israel," as they became known, faded from memory in the mists of complex history and social assimilation, while other people inherited their land.

Meanwhile, the situation in Judah was only slightly better. About half of its kings showed some interest in being true to the covenant, a few of them being reformers who restored elements of the law and worship of Yahweh. The other half promoted Canaanite ways, while the utmost Baal enthusiast among Judah's kings was a man called *Manasseh*. He rebuilt the sacred groves and other sites of Canaanite worship that his reforming father Hezekiah had destroyed, and he even placed a variety of foreign altars in the courtyards of Solomon's temple, with a carved statue of a Canaanite deity right inside the sacred building. Allowing human sacrifice in the land, Manasseh burned some of his own sons to death and practiced several Canaanite arts, consulting with sorcerers, mediums, and the like. Many of Judah's inhabitants followed his lead into these practices, so that it became known that Judah did more and went further in these things than even the Canaanites before them had done.

The Assyrians, now getting word that the Jewish God was displeased with the behavior of his people, decided the time was right to send armies to Jerusalem. They succeeded in this and carried off the Jewish king in chains. To everyone in Judah it was a warning that they were no more immune from the terms of the covenant than Samaria had been. Religion and temple would not protect them from the consequences of their actions. After two years under arrest, a chastened and repentant Manasseh was restored to his throne. He then undid many of his previous actions and died peacefully as a worshipper of Yahweh.

Nevertheless, the die was cast. Manasseh's heir immediately expressed his preference for Canaanite gods, though he reigned only a short time. Afterwards, his young son *Josiah* brought to Judah a short-lived revival of the faith of the fathers. A long-missing manuscript of the laws of Moses was found in the process of Josiah's repairs of the temple, and this "Book of the Covenant" was read to all the people while some of the old ways were re-instated. But Josiah was less astute in international affairs, making major errors in the politics of the region and dying needlessly in an ill-conceived battle against Egypt.

The land of the Nile then controlled the land of Judah until the rising power of Babylon swept over the whole region and came to the gates of Jerusalem. This new invader was the southern Mesopotamia nation of *Chaldea*, a longtime enemy of Assyria. It conquered Babylon to its north and just kept moving on as Assyria showed weakness. The prophet *Jeremiah*, seeing the Chaldeans coming toward Judah, strongly urged his nation not to resist them, saying that the approaching offensive was designed by God — but what a message this was for a proud people who trusted in Mount Zion and the temple! Jeremiah was bitterly opposed and reproached. His message went unheeded.

It was soon after 600 BC that the invaders arrived, taking away the king of Judah and all Jews except the poorest, forcibly removing them to the district of Babylon, the new Chaldean capital. Jerusalem's wall was breached and the temple was looted and burned down along with other important buildings. Jeremiah had been right all along but now it was too late. Not enough people had been willing to take his message to heart.

The nation of Judah was as good as destroyed. Within a generation or two its prophetic voices would cease altogether, and who then would remind people of a better way? To the inhabitants of Jerusalem and the country all around, the life that they had known was ending tragically. It was the first of several huge calamities to descend on the Jews and it was bound to have an effect on people's perceptions and beliefs. It wasn't very encouraging to me either as I felt I was now getting far into the "cave" of the search with hardly any more light than what was needed to proceed to the next stage just ahead of me. Then I reminded myself that this was, as I believed, an epic story with many long developments. I thought about that and moved on.

Chapter Eight
Facing the death of the past

1. New questions, new answers

Not only Samaria but also Judah had lost its valuable inheritance and independence, with all that these meant for their own culture. The nations where there had been some lingering Abrahamic spirituality had both been crushed. If the outlook of Abraham and his covenant had entirely failed at this point, it was likely that any faith along that line would now just be people's way of keeping some hope alive through religious practices. Such a stubborn or forlorn attempt at keeping it going after the collapse could sufficiently explain the inconsistency in Abrahamic religion. I would then have an adequate answer for the question of what had gone wrong with the outlook and covenant of Abraham, but not much hope for the future of its spirituality.

However, I wasn't ready to conclude my project yet, knowing there was much material still to consider. Whether this really was the beginning of the epic's end was something the documents would have to decide, but I was going to look carefully for signs that the documents from this point on were something more than Karl Marx's "opiate of the people" — in other words, religious techniques for escaping a terrible situation.

"Terrible" was probably an understatement. With the demolition of Jerusalem and the deportation of thousands to Babylon, the painful outcome of the repeatedly-broken national covenant was confirmed and made clear to every Jewish soldier, priest, parent, child, worker, newly-wed, and senior citizen. They mourned and cried about the disaster in their laments.

All the people moan because they seek bread,

> giving their valuables for the food that revives...
> Is it nothing to you, all you passers-by?
> Look and see if there is any sorrow
> like the sorrow inflicted on me...
>
> By the rivers of Babylon we sat down
> and wept when we remembered Zion.
> We hid our lyres in the willows
> when our captors called for amusement
> and said, "Sing us a song of Zion."

There was even more than deportation to deal with, for the calamity stirred up a lot of unanswered questions (at that time, and even now). Had God utterly rejected his chosen people, or had he lacked the power to prevent the impending disaster? Even if remnants of the chosen people now returned to Yahweh to really keep his law, how could the past be restored to them and the story just continue as if nothing much had happened? Their own kings had played a role in leading the nation into error, so what form of government could avoid the previous faults? In any case, and in the meantime, what was the attitude God would want Jews to have to their Chaldean captors?

A few remaining prophets, a handful who weren't ashamed to still be known as prophets, started providing some answers. The most respected man among them now was Jeremiah who had stood almost alone against many court seers and forecasters whose overly-confident predictions had all proved wrong. Jeremiah had been permitted by the Chaldean authority the freedom to stay in Judah, and from his new base away from Jerusalem the prophet set out his basic approach.

The calamity was Yahweh's doing, he said. It was the end result of many years of Judah's faithlessness amid the enticements and fierce ambitions of the nations. Yet in seventy years' time, Jeremiah promised, God was going to bless a remnant of the people by bringing them back from captivity. After that, Yahweh will make a new pact with them, a covenant different from the law-and-land arrangement of the days when Israel came out of Egypt.

At that later time, the emphasis was going to shift to individual faithfulness. No more would children pay for the sins of their fathers, because the law and knowledge of God would be written on each person's heart and the transgressions of the nation's past would be forgiven. In that distant time, a man would come who is called "the Branch," a righteous king of David's line. Until that day, the Jews were to try to live as normally as possible in Babylon, working for the prosperity of that city and for themselves, in anticipation of rebuilding in Judah.

Jeremiah's message was soon echoed by a young Levite named *Ezekiel,* called to prophetic service among the captives in Babylon. He also spoke of individual responsibility and salvation, of God's faithfulness to the dispersed remnants of the people, of a future return and a new kind of obedience from a new heart. To all that, Ezekiel added that resettlement in Judah would definitely not be a reward for a better keeping of the law but that Yahweh would simply act to honor who he is, not a failed tribal god but a great Power above all earthly powers.

This young prophet believed that Yahweh was sovereign in his plans and actions, using the nations to do whatever would ultimately suit divine purposes. That belief in God's sovereignty brought an international theme to Ezekiel's messages as he spoke about various countries in that part of the world. He used the name *Adonai-Yahweh* (sometimes translated by the term "Lord God" or "Sovereign God") to promote Yahweh as not just a national interest of the Jews but as Lord over all the nations.

Ezekiel was a very visionary kind of guy and his mental images were remarkable for their vivid (though puzzling) detail. The difficulty in understanding his writings has attracted many speculations of what he really meant, and there have appeared various ingenious interpretations featuring spaceships and visiting aliens. The prophet's colorful descriptions seem to invite such inventiveness.

A large portion of Ezekiel's written work portrays in detail a new Jerusalem temple in a new Holy Land, though a careful reading shows that the specifics are quite symbolic and do not refer to a literal building or place. Ezekiel seemed to want to say to the captives that their fond notions of "temple" and "Jerusalem" were going to have to be altered: they could get over their illusions about the loss of such things without remaining a disillusioned people.

One of the most intriguing aspects of the messages of Ezekiel and Jeremiah is that they contained much that was new to Jews of that day. This was anything but a rehashing of the old religion. Most people wouldn't have grasped the intended meaning, certainly not in the particulars but perhaps not even in the main themes. Did they really believe that their God had brought about world events and therefore also their own private destinies? Was his power to smite and end an era also his power to save and restore? The questions and answers were interesting and significant, but to many people they were also puzzling and uncertain.

Though these two prophets of the time of exile attempted to rescue people's faith by placing the Abraham covenant on a level larger and more international in scope than what Jews had been used to thinking, perhaps only time would tell what the truth of the matter was. Time was indeed the central issue: it was now clear to everyone that the clock of life refused to linger in order to please any person or nation. The world had changed a lot and would change some more. A new and doubtful age had begun, and the way that the people of Judah lived their beliefs would have to meet the challenge of the times.

2. Strange goings-on

About seventy years after the Babylonian captivity had started, the Chaldeans were overthrown by the Persians, bringing Jews their opportunity to go back to Judah. Emperor *Cyrus I* of Persia had already built a large domain on the borders of Chaldea when his troops took the city of Babylon without a battle, thus sparing the lives of all the exiles. Being unusually wise for a conqueror, the emperor's policy was to respect people's beliefs and to portray himself as their liberator from the oppression of previous rulers. In line with that policy, in the year 538 BC Cyrus ordered the return of the Jews to their homeland and provided for the rebuilding of their temple.

Two decades after Cyrus' decree, a priestly scholar named *Ezra* received royal authority to lead a group of exiles back and to appoint necessary local officials. His own authority would include being the official professor of law in Judah. In the course of this work, Ezra conducted a recompiling and editing of the Scriptures, basically the last major reorganization of its kind for the Hebrew holy books. The present form of the Jewish Bible is largely Ezra's doing — not that he made it up or completely transformed it, because the writings were already available and were held in very high regard.

In this work of editing as well as in other tasks, Ezra was assisted by the prophets *Haggai* and *Zechariah*, and together these men took up the challenge of building a new temple. They found it wasn't easy to ask the returned exiles to construct a temple when people were pioneering, being busy building up their own homes and fields from scratch. There was both quiet and vocal resistance to the proposed construction, but the project got underway with royal sponsorship.

As the temple work slowly progressed, Zechariah received a generous gift of silver and gold from some wealthier people in the land. And then he became rather secretive. No extra funds went toward the construction expense accounts, and within hours of the donation no one knew where the silver and gold had disappeared to. Judah was generally very poor and this liberal gift was sorely needed for the success of the temple work, but it had quickly gone missing.

That evening, Zechariah called some people together at a home in Jerusalem and he especially invited the young high priest *Yeshua* (the name is short for *Yehoshuah*, also abbreviated to Joshua). With a bundle of cloth in his hands, Zechariah set Yeshua in the middle of the home's courtyard.

Then to everyone's amazement, the prophet removed the cloth and revealed a brilliant crown of a simple two-layered design. Without further ado, Zechariah placed the crown on Yeshua's head and said in a loud voice,

> So says the Lord Almighty: Behold the man — "The Branch" is his name. From lowliness he will arise to build the house of the Lord. He will receive virtue to sit and rule on his throne and will be priest in his own right. Between both (offices) will be the counsel of peace.

Stranger still, as soon as he had made his speech, Zechariah removed the crown from the high priest's head and handed it over to the four people who had made the donation several hours before. They were dumbfounded, but he told them that the intention of their gift would be honored. The crown that had hastily been fashioned from their silver and gold would be kept inside the new house of God as a memorial to their pious generosity and to inspire others.

Coming from Zechariah the man, the symbolic coronation of Yeshua pointed to his hope that The Branch, the ideal priestly king who had earlier been announced by Isaiah and Jeremiah, would soon be sent to the nation. Coming from him as Yahweh's voice, the importance of the event lay in its renewed promise about a doubly-anointed member of the now defunct royal family, of someone who would be both a humble man of the people and a powerful king.

From this time on, the notion of the *Messiah* (in Hebrew: *ha-mashiach*, "the Anointed-One"), the meek advocate and mighty ruler, comes to the foreground of Jewish thinking and expectation. I am sure that some readers will immediately think of Jesus of Nazareth as the Messiah, but we should not at this point try to make such a leap. The epic has so far been altering and adding much to the understanding of Abrahamic religion and I expected, still apprehensively, that much more would be affected by the developing story. The understanding about a

Messiah, Jewish or Christian, would likely undergo change as well.

3. The new fundamentalism

Consider for a moment what you might have done if you had been a Jew in the time of the return from captivity. What would you have thought was most important to do and how might you have gone about the task? Then also consider how that would have been different from what actually took place.

Professor Ezra believed that it was now especially necessary for Judah to keep the law of the covenant and to hold to it more strictly than ever before. This could achieve greater legal faithfulness to God than prior to the Babylonian period, and that would presumably preserve the covenant blessing. In this effort, Ezra could tolerate no grey areas, no indistinct boundaries. He criticized the Levites and others in Judah for having married women who were not born-Israelites, women who possibly had been friends and neighbors in Babylon. He wanted them promptly to divorce each one. And Ezra was by no means alone in such strictness.

One day, some people came down from Samaria claiming to be Ephraimites, descendants of exiled Israelites who may have made their way back after the fall of Assyria. They and some of those other nations who had been resettled in former Israelite territory had turned to Yahweh apparently quite on their own. There is no record of the names of people who might have led such a noteworthy revival of Yahweh worship in Samaria, but during the absence of a temple in Jerusalem, the Samaritans had begun to have periodic sacrifices on the summit of *Mount Gerizim,* located beside the city of Shechem.

"We also are worshippers of the God of Abraham, Isaac and Jacob," they now said, "and have come to help build his house in Jerusalem."

The Jews would have none of it. They thought of Samaritans as the cursed offspring of covenant-breakers and idolaters, if not simply imposters from other nations. Under no circumstances could Samaritans be allowed to join in the temple's construction. To accept them as partners would defile the house of God and go against Ezra's plan to build a purer nation.

The high priest Yeshua and the other Levite leaders accepted this view of the matter, perhaps forgetting Hosea's prophecy of Samaria's return to its land and God. They made a firm decision with far-reaching consequences: bluntly and reproachfully they turned the Samaritans away. That straightforward rejection and scorn of their intentions insulted the Samaritans so much that, in a fierce reaction, they began strongly to oppose Jerusalem's temple.

Before long, another strict leader appeared, *Nehemiah* of Persia, "Cup-bearer to the King." This man was sent by a new emperor called Artaxerxes to repair Jerusalem's walls and gates. Nehemiah had his workers build with their swords beside them on account of threats and opposition to their work. The reconstruction was resisted by various Samaritans and other non-Jews living in the area, particularly people who originated westward in Palestine, as well as Ammonites and Arabs from east of the Jordan.

At long last, the walls of the city were closed in and completed, and then Nehemiah called all Judah together for a great eight-days-long feast. Ezra read the Torah, the laws of Moses, to the assembled crowd while priests went among the people to explain to them to the sense and implication of the words. Many Jews were in anguish to discover that they had known and practiced so little of the law, and they renewed the covenant at this time, having their names inscribed on a document of rededication.

The "Cup-bearer" then set out to enforce some key stipulations of the law covenant: barring commerce on the Sabbath day, ending debt-slavery, and forbidding marriage to foreigners. Nehemiah was particularly incensed at Jews who took foreign wives. "I argued with them and cursed them," he wrote in his memoir. "I hit some and plucked their hair, making them swear by God's name." He reasoned that mixed marriage was the very practice that had influenced even the wise Solomon with heathen notions — though he overlooked famous women of the faith such as *Ruth* a Moabite widow and *Rahab* a Canaanite prostitute, both of whom had become prominent ancestors in David's royal line.

Uncompromising, energetic and zealous, Nehemiah would not have ruminated long on such stubborn little facts. Quite sure of the righteousness of his cause and means, he zealously built the renewed nation into a viable entity. For better or worse, he set the tone of Jewish political and administrative leadership for many years to come.

4. *The last prophet*

With all this fresh emphasis on the Torah and its law as the way to develop the nation and keep it from repeating the errors that had led to captivity, there was one man who saw more deeply into the matter. His name was *Malachi* and he challenged his audiences and readers by telling them of a dialogue between them and God. It was a frustrating conversation, plausibly like some exchanges between a husband and wife:

> I have loved you, says Yahweh, but you say, "How...?"
> Priests, you have despised my name, but you say, "In what way...?" You also sneer and say, "How tiresome it all is..." You have wearied God with your words, yet you can ask, "How have we done this?"

Malachi exposed a lack of genuine, heart-felt respect for God, even in the act of worship. Though people were returning to the demands of the law, it appeared they had little appreciation for the concept that they were in a relationship with God. They looked for loopholes in the rules, doing as little as they thought they could get away with, such as offering at the temple the very poorest of their animals. God is great, protested Malachi, and is worthy of sincere respect among all nations.

Though Malachi is not well-known among the seers of Israel (achieving only limited fame as the last of "the minor prophets"), he spoke in the best tradition of Isaiah, Jeremiah and Ezekiel, pointing far beyond his time to a much different reality. He was able to promise hope despite people's lack of true understanding. There was no open criticism for his nation's strong focus on the law but he did say that something better was coming. "The Lord whom you seek will suddenly come to his temple — the very messenger of the covenant in whom (you say) you delight," and he will restore not the law but the relationship. Before the arrival of that great day, "Elijah the prophet" would come to teach them about relationship, turning the hearts of fathers and sons toward each other.

With those words, Malachi concluded his sensitive, insightful admonition. He was certainly applying the best of Abrahamic spirituality to the situation though it seemed too late to turn things around. When Malachi passed from the scene, the age of the Hebrew prophets came to a close and so did the Scriptures of the Jews, nothing more being added. From now on, Judah had to get along without any one who could speak the present words of Yahweh. The Hebrew Bible ceased to be a living book, though it was still read and consulted frequently out of a strong interest in the law, the land, and Israelite history. Some people would start to glance at other traditions and ideas for their view of life, but religious Jews would be looking to the past.

A fiercely-conservative era had dawned.

Chapter Nine
Brother against brother

1. Heart and soul

There was a socially important family that was torn apart by religious differences and romantic love. On one side of this family there was *Jaddua,* a deeply religious and earnest man who believed with all his heart that the errors of the past must not be repeated. On the other side stood *Manasseh* his brother, more given to romantic notions and having fallen in love with *Niki,* the beautiful daughter of a rich and powerful man.

Jaddua had inherited the position of high priest in Jerusalem, while Manasseh, in accordance with tradition, shared some of the daily religious duties with him in case his brother would be absent on account of illness or death. But many people were uneasy about Manasseh. Though priests were allowed to marry, the problem they had was Niki. She was a Samaritan, considered in Judah to be a foreigner and therefore not to be included in the covenant. Had not everyone since the days of Nehemiah been told to divorce foreign wives? Then why should Manasseh, especially on account of his role in the religious leadership of the country, not put his new wife away? This is what people were saying and Jaddua definitely agreed with it.

Manasseh brought this problem to his new father-in-law, *Sanballat,* an aging man despite having a beautiful young daughter, and a high official appointed as governor of Samaria by the emperor *Darius.* "I love Niki," Manasseh told the dignified governor. "I do not want to lose her nor the honor of the high priestly position that belongs to my family."

Sanballat was pleased to hear this, knowing that by marrying this man, Niki had the opportunity to build on his own success. "My son," he replied, "if they force you out of the priesthood for the sake of love, I will have Samaria accept you. We shall have in Shechem a high priest of true ancestry and the emperor himself will bestow the honor on you at my request."

Meanwhile in Jerusalem, the whole affair about Manasseh had thrown a light on all the priests and Levites, and it was found that there were not a few who had married Samaritan or other non-Jewish women. Crowds of people now swarmed into the streets, protesting the erring officials and demanding divorces or resignations. But others felt emboldened by Manasseh's stand to voice their opposition to the hostile strictness.

Sanballat looked for an opportunity to advance his plan. Using his money and prestige, he rescued the marriages of the more liberal priests and Levites by granting them land within Samaria. Moreover, it became known that the Persian emperor was soon coming to the region. Darius was traveling with a large army to meet a strong and so far successful invader from the Greek-speaking west, namely *Alexander the Great.* This would be the occasion to obtain royal support for a new official religion in Samaria, with Manasseh established as its high priest.

As it turned out, before the emperor could meet with his Samaritan governor, he was beaten in battle and fled back to Persia. But Sanballat was not beaten. Hearing that Alexander of Macedonia was now turning south to set his sights on nearby Tyre, the governor quickly mobilized an armed force and marched his soldiers to Alexander for his support. When the conqueror received him well, Sanballat said, "I have a son-in-law who is the brother of the high priest in Jerusalem, and he with many other Jews now living in Samaria want to have their own temple. It would be advantageous to you to grant it and thereby divide the Jews, for they have proved to be troublesome to whoever rules them."

Alexander gave his approval and agreed to protect Samaria with its new temple, which Sanballat then hastily built on Mount Gerizim, next to the historic city of Shechem. He established the official worship of Yahweh in the very location where Israel of old had broken off relations with Judah. Alexander meanwhile went on to complete his conquest of the Lebanon district and the Gaza strip, and then turned his armies toward Jerusalem.

2. How the great city was spared

Manasseh's brother Jaddua could not in good conscience switch allegiance the way Sanballat had done, for he felt the weight of a solemn oath he had made to emperor Darius. He told Alexander so in a letter but the conqueror was in no mood to grant clemency to this scrupulous Jew. Before long, he arrived in front of the gates of Jerusalem to punish it for this peculiar stubbornness. From the walls of the city, Jaddua watched the large host march closer and, with great anxiety, he urged everyone to join him in making sacrifices and to pray fervently for God's help in the face of this looming disaster.

That night, Jaddua had a dream. In it, he was told that the city should be festively decorated and its citizens should meet the conqueror in white garments of celebration, but that the priests should wear their appropriate robes and he his impressive high priestly attire. The dream seemed to be a divine message saying that, despite the oath, Alexander should be welcomed and not resisted, because his successes were part of God's sovereign plan.

Awakening, the priest took courage and put the dream into action, meeting the advancing Greek armies with a remarkably bold but peaceful procession. Priests and people walked in orderly fashion through the city gates and out to the approaching attackers. When a surprised and puzzled Alexander saw Jaddua clearly, he advanced alone towards him as his troops and all Jerusalem watched. Dismounting, he respectfully saluted the high priest with a deep bow. The other priests then gathered round and greeted the Macedonian hero.

Behind them, the hostile armies looked on bewildered, thinking that Alexander must have gone mad. An officer watching the strange scene quickly came near and said to his general, "Why do you worship their high priest when the whole world worships you?" The conqueror explained that it was not the priest but the priest's deity that he honored, for way back in Macedonia he had seen in a dream a man dressed exactly as this priest was. He believed that through this means God had shown him at that time that he should be strong and cross over quickly into Asia, where he would be given victory over the Persians.

He now called off the planned attack on Jerusalem and, newly inspired and encouraged, entered the city peacefully. At the temple, Alexander offered sacrifice to Judah's God according to Jaddua's instructions. Then he was shown the place in the book of Daniel where it was prophesied that one of the Greeks would destroy the Persian empire. Further heartened by this unexpected belief in his leadership, Alexander granted the Jews freedom to follow their law. He also exempted them from paying tribute during any Sabbath year when their lands were lying fallow, and these decrees the conqueror honored during the rest of his short life.

3. The deepest darkness

After the death of Alexander the Great, his empire was carved up among the chief generals, and their ambitions had no room for Alexander's promises to the Jews. During the ensuing years of back-and-forth warring among the divided successors, Judah and its neighbors suffered terribly. One or other king "Ptolemy" from Egypt in the south and some king "Antiochus" from Syria in the north fought against each other for dominance over the strategic corridor of land between the Jordan River and the Mediterranean Sea. One of the Ptolemies took many captives from Judah and Samaria, resettling them in Egypt to work for Egyptian-Greek masters. People who remembered the ancient writings must have been startled to recall the prediction made many centuries before by Moses that the breaking of the covenant would eventually lead Israel back to their original "house of bondage."

As matters grew worse, there came a time when a descendant of Jaddua was removed from the position of high priest by a

Pagan king. The priest was *Jason,* who had adopted this Greek name but in his own language he had borne the meaningful high priestly name of Yeshua (or Joshua). The Greek king of Syria who removed him was *Antiochus Epiphanes,* who believed himself to be divine. In Jason's place, he installed the priest's brother, generally called by the Greek name of *Menelaus.*

Jason, however, together with many supporters, strongly resisted the priesthood of his brother. Then Menelaus, feeling quite embattled, fled to Antiochus and made a pledge to the king that if he was restored to the sacred office, he would transform Jerusalem into a center of Greek culture, complete with a great sports gymnasium inside "the Holy City." Antiochus-the-God seemed pleased with this promised departure from Jewishness and soon appeared at the gates of Jerusalem, pretending to be on a peaceful visit. When he was welcomed inside, his troops ransacked the temple of Yahweh, stripping it bare of gold, money, ornaments, sacred vessels, drapery, and presumably also the prophetic double crown that Zechariah had made. Then Antiochus handed back the now impoverished priesthood to Menelaus, whose offer had apparently fallen short of the king's ambitions and pretensions of divinity.

As if this betrayal of his puppet priest was not enough, after a brief space of time the king returned to Jerusalem to pillage the rest of the city and burn many of its buildings. On this second occasion, Antiochus built at the temple an altar to his chief deity Zeus, sacrificed pigs on it (strictly forbidden in Jewish law), and then ordered that the same be done throughout all the villages and towns of Judah. He prohibited the law of Moses, especially the practice of circumcision, so that children who were circumcised after the publication of his order, and mothers who brought their sons for circumcision, were frightfully abused and killed in terribly brutal and torturous ways.

Many Jews obeyed the king's orders, probably out of fear but some also from agreement, for there were those who followed Menelaus and preferred the Greek lifestyle. People in Samaria likewise did a quick about-face. Suddenly denying any ethnic tie to the Jews, they accepted placing a Greek name on

Sanballat's Mount Gerizim temple to honor the Olympian god Zeus.

The situation was grim in the extreme. Most of Israel had disappeared except for the claim of some Samaritans to be Israelites, and though many Jews had returned from captivity, they had not regained full control of Judah. To top it off, the religion that defined their existence was now outlawed and brutally suppressed. How much worse could it get for them, and how long would it take until a genuine turning of the tide? Only a true prophet could tell, but there had been no such person since the days of Malachi.

4. *Zealous fire*

One day, a man called *Mattathias,* of the Jewish family of *the Hasmoneans,* refused the order to sacrifice a pig to Zeus. The hot blood of his Levite clan boiled over in him as he stood at the Pagan altar in the center of his village and said loudly, "I, my sons and my brothers, will follow the covenant of our fathers! May heaven keep us from forsaking the law and ordinances — we will not obey the king's orders!"

At that electrifying moment, as if not hearing Mattathias, another Jew quietly stepped up and began to sacrifice as the king required. Shocked and "fired with zeal," the other man threw himself at the worshipper and killed him on the altar. Mattathias then also slew the king's commissioner who was there to see to the sacrifice. He quickly destroyed the altar and ran through the town yelling, "Everyone with zeal for the law and the covenant, come out and follow me!" He fled, along with his whole family, leaving all their possessions behind.

Others soon joined him in the desert where they all lived in caves, planning their hasty strategy. Mattathias gathered a few thousand followers and as they began to perform many successful strikes on the altars, killing those who openly sought to break the Jewish sacred law, the fear of them spread through all the country round about. In a year's time, he was dead of an illness and his son *Judas Maccabeus* took over the leadership of the growing revolt.

Judas faced overwhelming odds as every army he had to meet was much larger than his own force. He was, however, passionate about the covenant and possessed useful oratorical ability:

> It is easy for a great number to be routed by a few! In the sight of heaven it is all one, whether by many or by few. Victory in war does not depend on the size the fighting force, it is from heaven that strength comes! ... We fight for our lives and our laws. God will crush them before our eyes! Do not fear them!

Judas and his forces were victorious again and again, even in the face of great odds. Within two years, he was able to march into Jerusalem to cleanse and rededicate the temple that had been left desolate since the attack by Antiochus. Now established in the holy city, the Hasmonean family, led by Judas and his brother Simon at the head of two armies, fought with opposing nations round about. Interestingly, they also entered into a mutual defense pact with *Rome,* for the extraordinary military successes of each side in this treaty had become known far and wide. Jewish diplomats, on their return from the journey to Rome to negotiate the agreement, made an invited stop at *Sparta,* as these Greeks seemed eager to persuade them that Spartans too were descended from Abraham! The name of the old father of the faith had begun to spread through the world.

In the second generation of the renewed independent Judah, the family member called *John Hyrcanus* became a very successful holder of the high priestly office and was loved by the people. John launched an attack against Shechem and much of Samaria, zealously laying waste the now 200-year-old temple that Sanballat had built. This destruction enforced the Jewish belief that Israel's God could only be rightly worshipped in Jerusalem, just as it cemented Samaritan resentment of the Jews.

John also conquered land immediately to the south of Judah, an area known as *Idumea,* settled by descendants of Esau, the brother of Jacob. John compelled the inhabitants to be circumcised and urged them to obey the whole sacred law. These Edomites or Idumeans adopted the Hebrew ways so well that it became common simply to refer to them as fellow-Jews. They came to be accepted even while the Samaritans remained rejected. Esau, at long last, was back in the covenant, and the old stories seemed more alive than ever.

For much of his life, John Hyrcanus belonged to the religious sect of *Pharisees* but was later persuaded to abandon them in favor of the *Sadducees.* Sadducees emphasized free will and believed that the law had a limited authority, being restricted to the Torah, the five books of Moses. Pharisees, on the other hand, believed in God's sovereign control and made room for a wider application of the law. They held that other Bible books also had regulating authority and they added many rules for daily life. There was also a third major group, the *Essenes,* the usual name given to a loosely-related set of rigorous sects that believed in a very detailed predestination. But John, as we noted, became a Sadducee and ruled Judah for thirty-three years.

5. A coming of eagles

Regardless of the religious conviction and courage of the earlier Hasmonean leaders, after John Hyrcanus it was downhill all the way. The experiment in holy government faltered as John's offspring, not always mentally stable, brought shame, disorder, and division. As if to cover their weakness, they blatantly crowned themselves as kings as well as high priests. When a surviving queen divided the offices again, making one of her sons king and the other high priest, the two sons quarreled for years. Coming to the aid of the priest was a wealthy Edomite/ Idumean called *Antipater* and together their forces besieged Jerusalem where the other son had the most power. It was Jewish civil war, brother against brother, and for a long while there was a stalemate as neither one was able to overcome the other.

Now it just so happened that the Roman general *Pompey* came into the region at this time with his army. Each side in the Jewish dispute, remembering their treaty with Rome, rushed off to ask for his help in their struggle. Pompey was at first wise enough not to commit to the quarrel, but when both sides continued to press for support he eventually made a decision and redirected his army toward Jerusalem.

Nearing the great city, Pompey made his intentions known. He had come to win Jerusalem on behalf of the high priest. When the battle was over the high priest got his quarrelsome sibling removed from office but did not get anything more. Pompey looted the temple as payment for the intervention and appointed Antipater, not the priest, as the new ruler in Judah. Thereby the Roman general, in effect, followed old Sanballat's advice to Alexander, shrewdly keeping Jewish loyalties divided into two different camps.

Yet so often, history moves on by acts of political convenience and expedience. Antipater switched his allegiance in order to help *Julius Caesar* get rid of Pompey. Having benefited from that unexpected support, Caesar then granted Antipater the rulership of both Judah and Galilee, making the man's two sons viceroys in these territories under Roman supervision. Soon thereafter, the son known as *Herod* became king of what Caesar called *Judea,* the extended old kingdom of Judah, now virtually a captive state under the Roman eagle.

Jacob had to stand to one side as the birthright returned to Esau. Herod and his family, being converts from Idumea, were considered to be members of the Jewish nation, but they showed as little interest in keeping to the covenant as their ancestor Esau had done. Herod did begin building a splendid expansion of the temple of Yahweh, but his personal morals and his strategies as king had no connection to Yahweh or the law of Moses.

The Samaritans, now without temple or political influence, chafed under a second-class status or worse, in a homeland that was governed by Herod and guarded by Rome. Likewise, the Jews generally had very little say in their government, even those who favored Herod. They began to show more interest in the *Sanhedrin,* the religious council composed of Sadducees and Pharisees, presided over by the high priest. Some other Jews became *Zealots,* aiming to destabilize the government and the Romans by acts of violence.

Such was now the divided and largely discouraging state of affairs in Roman Judea. People had seen several aspects of the epic re-appear but not deliver the full promise of the covenant, and few could shed any light on the reasons for the continued disappointment of Hebrew hopes.

A Kingdom for the Heart

A timely retelling of an ancient epic

The epic ends

Chapter Ten
Voices of change

1. Of a different spirit

It was drawing near to the annual Pass-over feast and the roads were starting to fill more than usual as many Jews were making their way to Jerusalem. It was customary for people to visit the great city for at least one of the year's new moons or religious festivals and Pass-over was one the greater holy times, commemorating Israel's liberation from slavery. The major commemoration this time would take place in the shadows of Herod's breath-taking, renovated and expanded house of God, a marvel of towers and ornamented walls that must have outdone the ancient temple of Solomon.

As was common, those who traveled to Jerusalem from greater distances had to overnight in the open, in barns and stables, or at a village inn along the way. And so one day, a few Jewish men went ahead into a Samaritan village to look for shelter for their larger group of travelers further back on the road. The good-natured innkeeper and other friendly residents, seeing that the men's money was good, were eager to help the travelers with whatever they needed. The usual polite questions were asked: "Where are you all from? How long will you stay? Where are you headed?" But when the men answered, the villagers changed their behavior abruptly. After a brief glowering silence, they hurled insults at the travelers. Turning the prospective guests away, the Samaritans withdrew their welcome and offers of help.

The travelers were galled at being rejected this way. By the time they came back to their group up the road, they had worked themselves into a fury. Angrily, they told the others about the ill-treatment. Some of those who heard then also grew indignant and one of them raged, "We should call down a curse on the village so no one will ever do business there again!" Another one replied, "That's right! Let's be like Elijah and call down fire from the sky to burn them up!"

The head of the group just sighed and started walking away. When asked why he did so, he turned to reprimand them for their immoderate comments. "You don't know," he said, "of what spirit you are." He then moved on and led the way to a different road and a different village, where they would simply try again to spend the night.

The opposing voice had been that of another *Yeshua,* this time a man whose Levite mother had married a commoner who, however, was distantly descended from the ancient royal house of David. Yeshua had been in Samaria a year or two before the unpleasant encounter of his friends, when he had passed by Shechem, near Mount Gerizim and the site of Sanballat's former temple. On that occasion, he had been resting alone at a roadside well when a woman came to draw water. He decided to ask her for a drink.

"Why do ask a drink from me?" she replied, recognizing by his accent that he was not from there. "I thought you Jews had no dealings with Samaritans like me." As she continued to converse with him, the woman grew more intrigued. She told him, "Our forefathers worshipped on this mountain but you Jews say that people should worship in Jerusalem."

Her statement reflected the historical controversy between Jews and Samaritans, rooted in David's centralization of worship, later promoted by Ezra upon Judah's return from captivity. Yeshua's reply, on the other hand, pointed to a new way that went beyond this old issue. "The hour is soon coming," he told the woman, "when you won't need to come either to this mountain or to Jerusalem to worship God the Father. True worshippers will worship the Father in spirit and in truth."

His words marked him out as an unusual man, especially in that era, and the Samaritan woman at the well recognized this. She went to her friends and neighbors to say that she may have found a prophet or even the Messiah.

2. The coarse cousin's contribution

Yeshua, of course, is better known to us by the Greek and Latin version of his name, as *Jesus*. The time had now come for me to investigate what was written about this Jew and to look at his life not as the start of a new religion but as a chapter of the epic story. I wasn't sure how my view of him would change by doing this but I could already see how previous chapters were providing a framework for this re-assessment.

This man was aware of his namesake, the other Yeshua who had been given Zechariah's prophecies about "The Branch," along with the double crown. Equally conscious of this was his slightly older cousin *John (Yohan/Iohannes),* who had gone preaching and baptizing, dressed in rough clothing in the style of Elijah. That was reminiscent of Malachi's prediction that this prophet would appear just prior to "the messenger of the covenant." John did not speak of himself as Elijah, though as Malachi had envisioned, he did try to focus people's attention on the need for reconciliation with God and with each other. His main message to the crowds who came to hear him in the wilds by the Jordan River was: "The kingdom of God is at hand, therefore repent." Then he had them go into the Jordan River to wash, as a token of their intent to get ready for the Messiah.

John's understanding of the kingdom was not what the Zealots or Hasmoneans had been thinking, and his view of its compassionate king was far removed from a Mattathias or Judas Maccabeus conquering land by the sword. Though John became well-known and had a loyal following, he told everyone that he was simply preparing the way for another person whom he called "the Lamb of God." This would be someone who would obtain forgiveness for the people so that they might have renewal within themselves and their relationships. That healing task would be more about individual emancipation and recovery, spreading through relationships, than it was about national salvation.

It was soon clear to me that in one sense there was no Jesus without a John the Baptist. It was John who opened up a new way to understand the Hebrew heritage about the kingdom. The great Jewish-Roman historian Josephus was also aware of John's importance, and the old documents we know as "the Gospels" strongly imply that it was John's vision and labor that redefined many people's beliefs and expectations. His preaching at the Jordan River provided them with a way to deal with the heavy disillusion of their present life and national predicament. John's message was an invitation to believe that God had not forsaken them and that the covenant promises would come true after all.

It is not known how often John as an adult had opportunities to discuss these matters with his cousin. The one meeting recorded in the Gospels shows John quite convinced that his own role was the lesser when compared to that of Yeshua. After being arrested by Herod, the baptizer questioned if the new kingdom really would be started by his cousin after all, but when John was beheaded Yeshua picked up where his kinsman had left off and began to travel with a group of disciples, proclaiming the same message: "Repent, for the kingdom of God is at hand." The special understanding these two men had of the kingdom became the basis for Yeshua's unique dealings with Samaritans and others who were rejected because of bloodline or lifestyle.

Yeshua's interest in the underdog showed in many ways. His view was that in this kind of world there were bound to be terrible offenses and victims' hurts. God as a good Father was very aware of it all, keeping track, and he would set all things right in due time. Even the little sparrow that falls to the ground is noted by heaven, Yeshua once said, and how much more noted were the sufferings of humans who are of far greater value than birds. Once he said that those who abuse young children would face such a firm judgment from God that they would find a quick death preferable.

When he wanted to give his fellow Jews an illustration of a righteous man, Yeshua told them a story about a good Samaritan, to teach them that whoever does what is right is righteous — regardless of ethnic origin or religious status. His thoughts about Jerusalem's rank and its splendid temple were less favorable. Though he acknowledged the temple as a house of prayer and worship, when the people with him were ogling its imposing architectural features he poured cold water on their enthusiasm: "Not one stone will be left upon another," said he, already speaking of the destruction of the new buildings. He advised them, "Watch that you're not too easily impressed."

Judeans would not have been very happy with these views but Yeshua and his group were not from Judea but from Galilee, a fertile district adjoining the northern part of Samaria. Originally part of Israel's northern kingdom, it had come to have a mixed population and it used to be called "Galilee of the Gentiles" by the Hasmoneans. Though by the time of Herod it had numerous Jewish settlements, Judeans looked down on Galilee only a little less than on Samaria. Moreover, of Yeshua's Galilean hometown there was a dismissive saying: "Can any good come from Nazareth?" Yet it was from here that John's cousin decided to launch his life's work.

3. The work begins

One Sabbath day, Yeshua went to his own synagogue and read aloud this extract from the writings of the prophet Isaiah:

> Upon me is the spirit of the Lord [Yahweh] who
> anointed me to tell good news to the poor. He has sent
> me to proclaim release to captives, and give sight to the
> blind, and set free the oppressed...

He spoke of a kingdom in which those with little or no hope could find real help and a new identity. As for others, people with the means to avoid much pain and despair — well, it just wasn't for them. "It is easier for a camel to go through the eye of a needle than for the rich to enter the kingdom of God," he claimed. Only those with few of the comforts and supports that people crave could appreciate this kingdom, but since even Abraham had been moderately wealthy, Yeshua added, "With God all things are possible."

What then was this kingdom? Was it a political Israelite territory, a social philosophy to challenge Rome's dominance, or just a fancy metaphor for a new religion? Not only Yeshua's enemies but also his own disciples were confused about it. Little by little, their guesses were shown to be inadequate, as indicated by a question of whether taxes needed to be paid. In his answer, he implied there were two kingdoms, two different realities, both legitimate in their own way, when he said, "Give to Caesar what is Caesar's and to God what is God's."

I saw that the kind of kingdom that Yeshua promoted was in line with previous hints of such a view by some prophets like Jeremiah, Ezekiel, and Malachi, and that it seemed to be the key to Yeshua's life and teachings. That evidence within the writings known as the Gospels appeared to validate much of my work of rediscovery, and showed a "Jesus" who was significantly different from the authoritarian, sentimental, conservative, mystical, or emotion-laden views of him presented by various Christian religions. It was now plain to see that many Christians and their churches might not much like this Yeshua of the epic.

4. Deadly controversies

During the years that Yeshua traveled with his disciples, four main controversies swirled around the man. There were objections to his *choice of company,* questions concerning his *healings,* debates about his *view of the law,* and incredulity over his *claim of greatness.* These controversies, divisive as they were, helped to define for others his understanding of a coming kingdom, that it was radically different from any more traditional views.

Yeshua was known for his habit of spending time with people whom others labeled as "sinners." Those he ate with included social outcasts, people suffering rejection for reasons connected with their occupations as prostitutes or as tax collectors for the Romans. To the scandalized religious folk "the Teacher" explained that he had come to call sinners who were able to repent and change like young children — these were the kind of people for whom kingdom citizenship was meant, not the religiously self-assured.

Much of his work involved healing the less-assured people of their various diseases and ill conditions, and he also "cast out demons." It is clear from a few of these instances that some of the conditions people believed to be demonic were what we today would call psychosis and serious mental illness, as well as some temporary loss of personal control such as an epileptic seizure. Yet at other occasions there was something weirdly different from these relatively common conditions. Some people were of the opinion that this healer was in league with the powers of darkness. In reply, he said, "If I expel demons by the finger of God, then the kingdom of God has come to you." The miracle-worker's awesome powers, whatever people may prefer to view them as, to him were an indication that the influence of the ancient Rival on Earth was about to be broken.

The man from Nazareth was also known to be active on the Sabbath, the Jewish day of rest, when no one was supposed to do any work. He gave many responses to those who charged him with breaking the laws of Scripture, but one answer summed up his whole approach to this issue. "The Sabbath was made for man," he declared, "not man for the Sabbath..." This put the whole sacred law in a new light and framework.

The Hebrew body of law and its many interpretations had become an intrusive web of regulations that took scholars years of study even to comprehend, let alone follow correctly. To ordinary people these laws were a burden imposed by those who did not lift a finger to lighten the load. In the coming kingdom, on the other hand, there would be a much simpler arrangement, with just one constitutional commandment for all: "Love each other."

Seeing the way that Yeshua viewed his mission and kingdom, it was easy to think of him as a heretic, as being so different from what much of Judaism had been before him that he stood outside of the heritage. This is how he is sometimes portrayed by people of varying persuasions. I could see this too, but it was my special project to take note of the developing theme of the epic, all the way back to its start with Abraham. That consideration shed a different light on the matter and made Yeshua seem to fit the flow of the epic quite well.

To Bible-believing students in Judea who were diligently looking for spiritual help, the Galilean once said, "You search the Scriptures because you think that in them you have eternal life, but those Scriptures testify about me, and yet you do not come to me to have life." Though there was law and guidance in the holy books, the real point was not those teachings themselves but rather the overall story in its meaning and benefit. This was much the same as what my project of the epic had been about, although according to Yeshua, the focus of the documents was ultimately himself as the hope for spiritual life.

That daring assertion reflected the fourth and probably most bitter controversy. Many of his contemporaries would have known that the phrase "Son of Man" was used in Hebrew documents for special people like the great prophets Daniel and Ezekiel, and that it was the title given in one of Daniel's prophecies to a particularly-favored man of God, namely the anointed Messiah or Christened-One (the Christ). This Son of Man (a son of *Adam* is the meaning here) would triumph over the Rival's pretended power on Earth. Boldly, Yeshua told his disciples he was that Son of Man, sent from heaven by the Father to crush the dragon's head, as it were, though it would strike his heel. He also claimed to be greater than the temple, greater than king Solomon, and even that he existed with God before the time of Abraham. "Who has seen me has seen the Father ... I am in the Father and the Father is in me."

Many people found the claims hard to swallow. Really, only mad persons and demagogues made such immoderate assertions — unless, of course, there was some proof that this one man really came from God. But Yeshua didn't think much of demands for specific proofs and signs. If they couldn't believe his words, "at least believe on account of the works I have done," he would say, though sometimes he referred them to an odd promise that he would rebuild the temple in only three days. No wonder some thought that the Galilean's success as a healer and spiritual teacher had gone to his head, and they spoke ill of him because of it. Others considered his assertions to be high blasphemy and wanted him to pay with his life.

"If only this good man wasn't filled with such grand delusions," some may well have thought, as many people over the centuries would indeed think. But there was no getting around it. The primary benefit of the kingdom in Yeshua's view would come to people through allegiance to only one great guide and benefactor, one "king" — namely himself. Even pious devotion to the Scriptures would not qualify someone for life in the kingdom! A strange religion this was, if indeed it was religion at all.

People were free to leave if they didn't like it, and many did just that. But to any who could accept him, he promised free release from the hold that the religious law and a broken covenant had on their lives and consciences. "Come to me all you who are worn out and burdened, and I will give you rest," he said in promising them a fresh start. "Take on the yoke I am in and learn from me … for my yoke will put you at ease and my burden is light."

The documents show that many of those he healed or who had been intrigued by his fame and personality, people who would have considered him "really cool," eventually turned their backs on him because they couldn't see him as "really great." They left him on account of the unusual claims he made about himself. A few stayed to become a small community of support for his work, and some others held him in esteem privately and quietly out of fear of the authorities.

5. *The last days of the covenant*

We now pick up where we were in the earlier part of this chapter when Yeshua led his thin-skinned little group of followers through Samaritan territory. When they had finally reached their destination of Jerusalem, he gathered them into a rented room to eat the traditional Pass-over meal of lamb. There he washed the disciples' dirty and dusty feet as an illustration of the practical love he had preached. He again spoke of his close identity to the divine Father and predicted his immanent departure: his flesh would be torn and his blood poured out. The clear implication was that he would be the Pass-over lamb to whom the solemn Jewish feast had pointed all these years.

Yeshua truly believed that he was to be the sacrifice to end all the sacrifices — that is, by his suffering he would end the need for having the sacred law. If he was right, the laws of Moses had run their course and the prophecies about an entirely new covenant would soon start being fulfilled, though that would scare or offend most every devoutly-religious Jew. After the memorial meal, the group sang a hymn and all walked into the evening air into the garden beyond the walls of the city, a place known as the Mount of Olives.

Late that night, armed temple guards (not Roman soldiers) discovered them there and arrested him as his followers scattered. This scene and those immediately following are familiar to most of us, having seen them depicted in movies and plays. Even those who have never opened a New Testament can recall the scandalous night-time judicial hearings and the form of Jesus standing cut and bleeding before the Roman administrator Pontius Pilate, saying, "My kingdom is not of this world, or else my followers would have fought to prevent my arrest..."

Pilate had been intrigued with that statement. "You are a king then."

The prisoner answered, "You said it. This is the reason I was born and for this I came into the world, that I might testify to the truth. Those who are of the truth listen to my voice."

Pilate turned away, perplexed and irritated (as shown by his famous line: "What is truth?"), but nevertheless gave his judgment that the man before him was innocent of any charge. After having the accused flogged and beaten to appease the prejudiced crowd, Pilate pleaded, "Behold the man," and repeated his earlier judgment of innocence.

By this time, however, the crowd had a very ugly spirit. The

Roman could have dispersed the throng with a single order, for he had shown himself capable of ordering killings even in large numbers, but someone shouted that if Pilate released the man who was said to be a king, he would be no friend of Caesar.

Pilate feared Caesar. Some years later, after savagely attacking Samaria, he would be removed from office and sent to Rome for a hearing in Caesar's court, but would commit suicide before the proceedings could begin. Right now, Pilate reversed his decision and sent Yeshua off to die a tortured death by crucifixion. To identify the victim among several others who would have been hanging on crosses that day, a trilingual sign was fastened onto Yeshua's cross. It read (as translated from the Greek part) "Jesus the Nazarene, king of the Jews."

The documents show that not all the religious leaders in Jerusalem had wanted him dead, and it is certain that the call for his crucifixion did not come from Jews in general (the night-time crowd insisting on his death had likely been hand-picked for that purpose). Yet the voice of this most unusual man, Yeshua of Nazareth, was silenced. The one who had spoken of a different approach to people and to spirituality, who had pointed to a radically new order (even if some of it was hard to come to terms with) was gone.

Whatever one may think of the religions that were formed in his name or of deeds done by those who worship him, few people in Yeshua's own day saw what he saw, understood what he understood, and spoke as he spoke. He died relatively quickly, well before sundown the same day that he was nailed to the cross.

Chapter Eleven
Questions and explanations

1. *The road of doubt*

It was plain to see in the person of Yeshua a return to a spiritual outlook, distinct from an approach heavily mixed with political, legal, or technique-based interests. His view of the kingdom of God, like that of John the Baptist, was not aimed at gaining control of a society by government or army. All this was certainly something like the spirituality of Abraham, and the Gospels showed continuity with the epic's previous development as well as having new features.

My question now was simply: *could it last?* After all, what happened to Yeshua's teachings and outlook? When there is some mention today of the Abrahamic faith why do we tend to think of religions, world politics and warfare, instead of Yeshua's spirituality? Things still did not quite add up and further investigation was needed. The epic could not end with the death of this man.

It was already obvious that the ancient documents assume spirituality to be real, and that out-of-the-ordinary experiences form a part of the world's reality and of people's personal histories. Continuing to go with the flow of the epic, I had to stay fairly close to the way it appeared in the written sources, and at this point in the story, the writings were mentioning Yeshua's resurrection. The question I had to find an answer to was not "Did he really rise from the dead?" because that is a matter of trust and faith. "He lives in my heart," is what believers say. My inquiry was rather this: "Is Yeshua's resurrection a necessary part of the epic story?"

The answer to that second question would decide if, like many others details in the ancient sources previously, the resurrection was left out or put in the book. I thought it through, and on balance I had to conclude that the documents showed that the resurrection played a very large a role in the story from here on. If I continued to treat the documents fairly, it could not be edited out.

Nevertheless, after Yeshua's death, his followers were in the grip of the pain of confusion and shock. According to the written records, in the days immediately following the crucifixion the disciples had no encouraging or comforting answers, and certainly nothing about rising from the dead. Three days after the crucifixion, a couple of down-hearted disciples were on the road again, despondently walking away from Jerusalem to return to their old life in the village or on the farm. As they talked, they tried to make some sense of the recent distressing events.

"How could we have been so wrong?" said the one.

"I don't know," answered his companion, "but I think of the time when some theologians brought a woman they had caught in the act of adultery. They challenged the Teacher to say what his new way would do with her because the law of Moses required death by stoning. Yeshua answered them, 'Whoever is without sin among you, let him cast the first stone.' So one by one they all slinked away, didn't they?"

"I do remember it, and also that he then said to her, 'I don't condemn you, you can go, but don't do this sin anymore.' He seemed so good and so right, but God let him die a criminal's horrible death instead of leading him to establish the new kingdom! Where do we fit that in?"

Something along this line the two travelers were saying to each other when a stranger walking on the road came up from behind and asked what they were discussing. They told him all the disillusioning events that had taken place in the city recently, and how some women disciples had gone to the gravesite just that morning to find Yeshua's burial place shockingly empty. The stranger chided them gently and explained what Moses and other prophets had said about the Messiah, how he had to suffer and die before beginning his reign.

The stranger was a man who, when they had a good look at him, turned out to be none other than Yeshua himself, and when he disappeared from their sight like an apparition, the astonished men ran back to Jerusalem to the place where other disciples had gathered. On arriving, they blurted out the event on the road but were predictably met with skepticism and rejection from most of the others.

While they were arguing about it, Yeshua suddenly appeared in the room. Startled and scared, everyone backed away, some thinking they were seeing a ghost. But he let them see how his hands and feet had been pierced with nails and encouraged them to touch him in order to prove that he was flesh and bone. Then he asked them for something to eat, and warily being given a piece of fish, ate it in front of their flabbergasted faces.

The present indisputably-physical reappearance could not be ignored. It cast a new light on the Teacher and all he had done in the previous years. Some disciples now recollected that on various occasions he had said that those who believe in him would also rise after death. As deaf to those words as they had been, from this day forward a belief in the resurrection became a necessary part of their story.

2. *A new beginning*

According to a physician of the time, a man named *Luke,* Yeshua appeared to several audiences after his crucifixion. Others talked of seeing him quite recently in Galilee where he had addressed as many as five hundred people. Though these appearances seem to have been brief and there is little testimony of what was specifically said at them, it was significantly recorded that he "spoke about the kingdom of God."

The Teacher did not stay for long and on the final day with his closest group of disciples, he instructed them to wait in Jerusalem for a special counselor who would teach them in his absence and empower them to speak to others. Like Moses, he would leave them without hope of finding, and someone else would lead them into what was promised to them. So, when their master and friend had departed for the last time, the disciples returned to the big city with their horizons broadened.

Seven weeks after Pass-over, there was another festival in Jerusalem, the harvest holiday called the Feast of Weeks. While much of the northern hemisphere links harvest time with autumn, in hot and dry countries like Judea summer was not naturally a time of much growth, therefore the first harvest celebration took place in late spring. At this celebration, according to the doctor Luke, the disciples were gathered together in a house when, at about nine o'clock in the morning, the place was filled with a loud sound like a strong rushing wind. A bright fiery light came into the room and separated into smaller lights that settled on each of them, maybe somewhat like the haloes of later Christian art. When the disciples, unhurt, found themselves speaking in languages they hadn't even learned, they ran out into the streets with their new ability.

It wasn't long before Peter stepped up to address an assembling crowd with his explanation of the event. He quoted a prophecy of Joel: "…on my servants, both men and women, I will pour out my Spirit in those days…" Then he went on to talk of Yeshua's death and resurrection, ending with this sentence: "Let the whole house of Israel know for a certainty that God has made him Lord and Messiah, this Yeshua whom you crucified."

Many in the throng were moved by the speech and called out, "Brothers, what are we to do?"

Peter answered, "Repent, be immersed in forgiveness, and you will receive the gift of the Holy Spirit, for now the promise is to you, your children, and to any who may be far away, as many as the Lord our God may call."

Large numbers of people were baptized that day as a sign of faith and forgiveness. They remained close to the small following that had been at Yeshua's side for the past three years, as these men now instructed them and performed various healings. Voluntarily, many of the converts sold their own possessions and from the money raised gave to those who were in need.

This is how Luke described the momentous start of the

Christian movement, at first called "The Way." Whatever people in our highly technological society may think now, in that faraway time in Judea the number of persons grew quickly who newly believed in the resurrection and the presence of spiritual power — and that is a necessary part of the overall story.

3. The tale of a martyr and a persecutor

So rapidly did the number of resurrection-believers grow, that strong opposition was aroused. Members of the Sanhedrin council led the resistance to the new beliefs. After they conducted a quick trial, they personally participated in the stoning of *Stephen,* the first Christian spokesman to die as a martyr. At this execution, a young man named *Saul,* an intelligent and very strict Pharisee, held the cloaks of the councilors so they could take better aim. Young Saul's blood was stirred and he left the horrid scene caught-up in making murderous threats against The Way. In his youthful zeal, Saul went from house to house with others like himself, dragging away people to be imprisoned for religious offenses. A great persecution broke out and many who believed in the resurrection fled Jerusalem.

According to his contemporary biography, one day Saul was on the road going toward Damascus to arrest followers of The Way when a bright light flashed suddenly around him. He fell to the ground. A voice said this was Yeshua of Nazareth and told him to continue on into the city where he would be shown his next step. Some of those with Saul also heard the voice but saw nothing unusual, while others only heard what sounded to them like thunder. When the young persecutor got up, he was unable to see and had to be led by the hand the remaining distance to Damascus.

In the Syrian city, he was met by a Christian who bravely came up to speak with him, and during the course of that conversation Saul regained his sight as suddenly as he had lost it. Immediately he asked to be baptized, thereby becoming the movement's newest and most unlikely convert. As the years would show, he was also its most famous and influential one.

In due time, Saul (named for his tribe's famous son, the first king of Israel), altered his Hebrew name to the Greek-sounding "Paulos," which we know as *Paul*. The change reflected what he had become, for in the severity of his conversion experience he lost all the advantages he had been born into and had wanted. From being a devout, educated, up-and-coming zealous Pharisee, he became a life-long object of persecution, hated by his countrymen as being a turncoat, but he was also regarded suspiciously by those who believed in the resurrection. Again we have here a leader who, like Abraham and Moses, turned away from social status and its pursuits to follow a different drummer.

4. *Turning the world upside down*

Many have questioned whether Paul ever really understood Jesus, but at least right from the day of his conversion, he clearly knew that in Yeshua's kingdom no one had reason to boast of educational, ethnic, social, or moral superiority. He had experienced religion being turned on its head, for the religious core value of "righteousness" (being right and doing right) had proved to be misleading and unreliable. When he thought he had been vigorously doing God's will, Paul had actually done little more than vent his spleen and covet a leading role for himself.

It now seemed to him that those who were first in a spiritual sense were last in religious self-confidence. No longer convinced of his moral superiority, he started calling himself a great sinner (actually "the chief of sinners") for having been a violent oppressor. To those who may have idealized him as a celebrity convert, Paul spoke not of his exceptional gifts or strengths but of ordinary human weakness:

> I don't know what I am accomplishing because I do
> things I don't want to do, and the very things I hate,

> these I end up doing ... I find then that it is a given,
> that for one like me who wants to do good, evil is close
> at hand.

No longer did he avoid admitting that he was part of the common human race with all its peculiar weakness of character. Instead, firmly believing that Yeshua had set him free from the sacred law, it was now safe to give up the attitude of moral superiority and begin to look at himself more accurately. It was not that he thought the law to be something bad; on the contrary, he understood it to be good and holy, but it was ineffective. The law had been powerless to change human nature for the good and therefore it ultimately condemned the whole human race.

Fortunately, to Paul's mind, the sacred law had ended with Yeshua's death. This had been the sacrifice to end all sacrifices so that now a new approach was called for. People still had grave faults even without the law to point them out, but there was "now no condemnation," no basis for any judgmental attitude for those who accepted the meaning of Yeshua's sacrifice. In spiritual matters, the human heart was no longer something to judge for degree of faith but instead something to reach out to. He didn't have to get angry at others anymore for their not being sincere enough, right enough, or effective enough for him. What did it matter? As long as God was true, everyone else could be a liar. Issues of worship and spirit were becoming issues of relationship, and the new kingdom was veering away from the troubled, older religious regime.

Certainly these were unusual and radical views for that time, and they are still not consistently held in today's Abrahamic religions. It was inevitable that these ideas would be seen by many shocked believers as destroying morality and the importance of religion in society. But Paul didn't gain his freedom by snubbing God. Though rebellion against church or temple has often gone hand-in-hand with a rejection of a belief in a personal deity, Paul thought he had been given the one way to be personally free but also a firm believer. This view led to many misunderstandings with other people but he remained adamant about this important aspect of his gospel.

For Paul, Yeshua was humankind's highest representative as well as the clearest image of God, someone who had the authority to make the great creative changes. Of special interest to my search was the fact that in explaining his views, Paul went back before the time of the law, *back to Abraham.* In that understanding, Yeshua's work had made it possible for the blessings promised to Abraham to be fulfilled. The era of the law had been a necessary development at the time but now it was seen as an interlude. All things having to do with the covenant would be transformed and made new.

If, then, the era of the old law was passing, the time for the institutions based on that law was fading as well. Those institutions included the temple with its various sacrifices, and the theocratic state with its pretensions of acting for God. Freedom from the old law would also mean freedom from the old kind of kingdom. The new spiritual kingdom denied the present validity of "one nation under God" in any special sense and moved a restored paradise, a heaven-on-earth, well into the future, at the end of time.

5. *The difficulty of being free*

Paul had a fragile physical condition, quite possibly poor eyesight, which was quite a trial to him. He prayed that he might be made better but found instead that he had to be content with the inner strength of accepting his weaknesses. This belated apostle learned to say the subtle but meaningful words, "When I am weak, then I am strong," coming to accept suffering for himself even as he once had inflicted suffering on others.

At times, his leadership on these issues placed him at odds with leading apostles such as *Peter (Cephas/Simon),* whom he admonished publicly for slipping back after breaking with the discriminating tradition of not eating with Gentiles. Likewise, Paul's views were more clear-cut than those of *James (Iakobos/ Jacob),* whose Jerusalem-centered ministry had temporarily influenced Peter's behavior. There would be no "old boys' network" here. Wherever Paul went in his several journeys around the rim of the Mediterranean Sea, he became the Great Leveler for his insistence that in the new way, people are not given preferential or discriminating treatment as "Jew or Greek, slave or free, male or female," because all were one when they were in Yeshua's kingdom.

The apostle of the heart-set-free ran into fierce opposition almost everywhere he went. Some Greeks scoffed at the notion of resurrection and said Paul was nothing but a "seed-picker," a man who lazily used isolated scraps of ideas. Jewish audiences, on the other hand, were often aghast to hear from him that they were now on the same level as any uncircumcised Gentile and that Yeshua was greater than Moses. There were always those who were ready to heckle him or to charge that he was encouraging lawlessness with his "gospel of free grace."

To his accusers Paul replied that people can live by thanksgiving, so that being "free from the law" did not mean becoming "lawless" in behavior. Rather, it meant doing things from the heart and by a new spirit, because one wants to, from a deep sense of gratitude and not by compulsion. To the convert there was no longer a frowning divinity to appease with sacrifices and fearful obedience, but rather, God was a nearby friend to talk to, to appreciate, to love, and always to thank.

The changed mind of Paul poured out many such groundbreaking concepts. Sadly, however, there were occasions when he returned to flashes of ungraciousness and times when he made some petty negative judgments and questionable rules. The voice of liberty and grace was still capable of inciting a loud disagreement with friends through some narrow stubbornness of his own.

My earlier question was not yet answered. It wasn't clear that the new spiritual way could last in an unpredictable human race. If even someone of Paul's caliber and influence could at times be so inconsistent as to provoke an ungracious argument with close friends that led to their parting, what could one realistically expect from more ordinary mortals? Certainly in Paul's own day, no one could yet know whether the themes of freedom within genuine relationship, of faith and hope and love, could overcome the older mindset of law, religious superiority, judgment, and land. It remained to be seen if the new spiritual way would come through the fires of testing.

Chapter Twelve
The struggle to be

1. The birth pangs

Many people have heard of the famous book of "The Revelation," also known as "The Apocalypse," which has gone through stages of popularity from time to time with its highly symbolic and visionary language about dragons and angels, bowls of wrath and "666." The strange book speaks of a prolonged attack by strong evil forces and warns that the spiritual kingdom on Earth will not grow easily by means of triumphal parades and militarism, or even by well-informed popular support. Instead, the kingdom will come into its own only after many terrifying desolations, the beginnings of which Yeshua had once called "the birth pangs."

The pangs began in the years leading up to AD 66, when an emperor in Rome ordered that his statue be placed in every temple of the empire so that all people could worship him. The idea was acceptable to Romans and most Pagan religions but Jewish authorities sternly refused to follow the order. Consequently, the Jerusalem temple and Judaism were subjected to many humiliations by Roman soldiers and officials. This vicious pressure came to a head when Florus, a Roman administrator who had "filled Judea with abundance of miseries," stole large quantities of money and silver from the temple. That was too much for the long-suffering worshippers who had donated most of the money. They rioted in the streets in such considerable numbers that they overran the Roman garrison in a pitched battle.

King Agrippa and his sister Bernice, the last of Herod's line, had always cooperated with Rome and were sympathetic to Paul. Neither of these policies had earned them much respect with their Jewish countrymen, and when the garrison was captured by rioters the royal pair fled Jerusalem for their own safety. The entire city then fell into the people's hands. This sudden total victory, hardly what even the steamed protesters had expected, greatly encouraged the militant Zealots whose numbers now began to soar.

In order to quell the growing revolt, the empire sent over a large fighting force. Beginning in Galilee, Roman legionaries gradually worked their way down to Jerusalem, though early in this conflict great siege works had already been put in place to seal up the city. It turned out to be an especially ugly war. Jews by the hundreds of thousands were killed, some in battle, many others by crucifixion. Meanwhile, inside the besieged city the misery and hunger grew so great that a mother, pressed horridly to act against nature, slew her infant son and roasted him. Amid the extreme circumstances, leaders in Jerusalem fought among themselves, and any spokesman who advocated a way out by moderation and compromise, was murdered.

Imperial troops eventually breached the walls in the year 70 and entered Jerusalem in a bloody orgy of destruction. Nearly the whole city was burned to the ground, including the temple whose sacred vessels were carried off to Rome as booty. By the end of the year 73, the last strongholds in Judea were all captured, including the mountain citadel of Massada where many of the Jewish defenders committed suicide rather than surrender. These "birth pangs" had a lasting impact on Judea's relationship to the empire.

2. *The crushing blow*

The Great Revolt, as the uprising of these years is called, had turned out to be a massive disaster for the Jews, and yet the short-lived victory had given some people an appetite for more. Just three decades later, a Second Jewish-Roman war erupted when Jews in Libya started an insurrection that spread to Egypt, up the coast to Judea and all the way to Mesopotamia. In the course of the revolt, many Pagan temples were burned and large numbers of Greeks and Romans were massacred, thereby making the Jewish name odious to citizens of the empire everywhere.

Roman troops managed to contain the unrest this time as well, at the cost of Jewish lives, but despite the second defeat, less than twenty years afterwards a third Jewish uprising began as militant zeal remained alive. This time the revolt was headed by a man whom many Jews considered to be the Messiah. His name was *Simon bar-Kochba.*

In the year 132, bar-Kochba began the new rebellion. Unlike the previous attempts, this was a well-planned and intelligent effort, and he met with great success. For two-and-a-half years his victories enabled him to rule as Messiah and Prince of Israel over the territory of Judea. Forces under his command seemed unbeatable but Rome was not about to let him become an inspiration to other Zealots and patriots in various parts of the Roman world. It sent out against him no less than twelve armed legions, half of all the empire's fighting forces in existence!

The enormous show of Roman strength gradually wore down bar-Kochba's determined fighters and their ultimate defeat was as utterly brutal and devastating as it was predictable. Fifty fortified Jewish towns and nearly a thousand small settlements were completely destroyed. Over half-a-million Jews lost their lives and many were exiled or sold into slavery, bringing the total Hebrew casualties in the three wars to about one million dead and hundreds of thousands deported and enslaved.

The misery of the Jews was crushingly severe. Belatedly, they had to admit that bar-Kochba had been a false Messiah, though even the leading Hebrew teacher of that time, Rabbi Akiva, had once been convinced of the man's divine mission. No significant Jewish revolt took place again for over two centuries, while the heartland of Judaism shifted away from the thoroughly devastated Holy Land, to rise again in Galilee and Babylon.

Except for sporadic skirmishes, Hebrew leadership and religion now discarded the whole notion of armed revolt. Rabbinic instruction in the synagogues grew much more cautious and made spiritual applications of the messianic hope, not unlike the kingdom teachings of Yeshua of Nazareth whom they had not been ready to follow. The older land-based concept of the holy kingdom had been dealt one stunning setback after another and now went into a deep sleep — at least among Jews. Over the centuries to come, despite many occasions of being harassed by others, the Hebrew community remained largely peaceful and the rabbis tended to interpret hardships as the necessary experience of the Chosen People.

3. According to the whole

There were also birth pangs for the Christians. Many of their leaders died a violent death, including crucifixion, at the hands of those who opposed them. There are various legends of the lives of the apostles and while it's not possible to say how factual each one of these stories is, a general picture has emerged of a group of leaders working tirelessly and fearlessly to bring to others the news of the resurrection and the spiritual kingdom. Peter and Paul worked among Greeks and Romans as well as Jews, while the apostle Thomas seems to have gone as far as India. Egypt claims the writer Mark, Spain believes that Yeshua's brother *Sant'Iago,* also called *San Diego (James/ Jacobus),* ministered in their country, and other nations have similar legends.

Now with such large distances between Christian centers in the ancient world, one might expect several different kinds of Christianity to develop almost immediately, but some factors opposed such a development. Quite early on, Christians seem to have believed that the truth about the kingdom was known to all the apostles and their associates. Even Paul, not having lived with the core group of disciples during Yeshua's time, went to Jerusalem to check his understanding with the leaders there — "lest I was running (the course of my life) in vain," as he said. The "pillars" of the very young movement heard him out and concurred with the things he was teaching.

So there was a straightforward standard of truth among

Christians of those days. It was simply: agreement with the teachings of the whole group of leaders who had known Yeshua. These teachings consisted of the basic tenets of faith that were shared by all the churches. That important idea of "according to the whole" (in Greek: *kat'holikos,* from which the word "catholic" is derived) was professed in several statements of belief drawn up in the various centers. These statements all sounded much like the "Apostles' Creed," a summary of accepted teachings that later became the norm among Christians. Many of those early creeds included the sentence "I believe one holy catholic church" — or in other words: "I hold to a unified, rightly-distinct body of people whose beliefs are according to the whole." Sometimes the phrase "the communion of saints" was added, meaning the relationship and fellowship of all who believe, *regardless of secondary differences.*

The public statements or creeds were written so that people about to be baptized could better understand the faith of the apostles, and also because there were converts with other beliefs. Those differing beliefs were often more in keeping with the then-popular "mysteries," which were groups who claimed to have secret, exclusive knowledge that could only be received through initiation rites and subsequent stages of teaching. Several newly-written versions of the life and ministry of Jesus appeared in their circles, each believed to be the secret teachings that he had revealed only to a select few.

I had a closer look at these and read parts of various hidden gospels even though I suspected that they were blind alleys in my search.

There was a revival of interest in my time in the secret teachings of the ancient era. For people who sensed that Christianity had long gone astray, the idea of suppressed secrets about Jesus held a special appeal. I soon found, however, that though the hidden teachings used language similar to what Paul had used, they were too much of a break from the epic. The interest in hidden truth as opposed to publicly-proclaimed gospel, and the supposed superiority of a small class of "Gnostics" ("those who know" the secrets) as distinct from the communion of all believers, was rejected by most early Christians. The apostle John, after all, had written an entire epistle against the danger of such an elite getting hold of people's trust and freedom.

It turned out that a few of the secret doctrines taught an extreme kind of spirituality, as if nature and the body did not matter or even that these were evil. Possibly such teachings could lead to the renouncing of riches and worldly possessions, though they also led some early Gnostics to say that Jesus only seemed to have had a body and that he did not really suffer on the cross. One version even had "the real Jesus" standing invisibly beside the cross, laughing at his tormentors' attempts to make him suffer. This view may have been meant to encourage people to rise above their hardships but in doing so it made the Galilean's sacrifice of his life "immaterial," in both senses of the word.

I came to suspect that the fascinating, romantic and mysterious approach of the Gnostics was rejected by most early Christians, not because they submitted to some conspiracy among the leaders, but more likely just because the faith of "the whole" was more open, available to all, and gave them a voice in their own salvation.

4. *Holding to the kingdom*

It was therefore with the broader, "catholic" understanding that most Christians faced the birth pangs. Local bullying took place almost right from the start, leading to a dreadful five-years-long attack on Christians by the mentally-unhinged emperor Nero, who had them killed in Rome by mass crucifixions, burnings and other "most exquisite tortures," as the Roman historian Tacitus described it. Later emperors also sometimes found followers of the Nazarene a convenient target for distracting the disgruntled populace, though the means of murdering the victims sometimes differed according to region. The ancient Christian historian Eusebius said that roasting was preferred by persecutors in Antioch, in Macedonia it was asphyxiation by smoke, in Arabia axes were used, in Egypt body parts were cut off, and some areas of Greece tried to win this macabre contest of cruelty and indignity by scraping off the skin or hanging women naked upside down by one foot as sport for the voyeurs of the audience.

Though there must have been private outcries about these unjust abuses of power and the horrifying, almost demonic brutality, the Christians' trials seem *not* to have raised the objection of how a good God could allow this to happen to his own people. The persecuted faithful appear to have overcome their mental anguish by a strong belief that death was not the end nor was it the worst tragedy, and also by thinking that fortitude in their Christ-like affliction would honor their faith and their God.

Not all Christians in the empire faced intense physical punishment for their faith, and periods of persecution were seldom widespread. Still, the possibility of great suffering was always there and many believers were convinced, like Paul, that though the outward nature was being ruined, their inner selves were renewed day by day. The time of affliction in any case was seen to be short and "not worthy to be compared to the glory that will be revealed," especially considering the huge span of eternity. Rather than let the abuse push them too deeply into agonizing, depressive or angry thoughts, many Christians accepted the fact of pain and set their minds on winning a glorious resurrection. In this new view, the aggressive forces of evil were actually losing the battle (hence their phobic cruelty) while those who followed Yeshua/Jesus were on the brink of the victory of eternal life.

One day, in the arena at Smyrna (a city in Turkey), eleven Christians had been fed to the lions, causing the bloodthirsty crowd of spectators to get so excited that they called out for *Polycarp*, the senior pastor. When the aging believer was made to appear, the Roman proconsul, ruler of that area, told the old man, "I will set you free if you curse Christ."

The energized audience ceased their noise in order to hear his reply: "Eighty-six years have I served him and he has done me no wrong."

A great cry went up that the lions should be loosed but the proconsul was not ready to do this. "Then swear by Caesar's godhood!" he demanded.

Polycarp answered, "Since you pretend to be ignorant of my character, know that I am a Christian."

"If you do not change your mind," the other man warned, "you must be thrown to the wild beasts!"

The old pastor looked him straight in the face and said, "Let them come on." When the proconsul threatened to burn him alive, he answered, "Your fire will be spent in an hour but that which is reserved for sinners is eternal. Dispose of me as you please."

The old man was tied to the top of a pile of wood. He looked to the skies and prayed, "Blessed are you, O Father, that you made me worthy to partake with the holy martyrs the cup of Messiah's suffering, that my soul and body may be reunited in eternal life." Then the wood was set on fire and he departed Earth in a blaze. Both Christians and persecutors long remembered the vigor of his testimony in death.

5. Feet of clay

The empire's butchery of Jews, Christians, and some other groups of people, revealed the clay in the iron feet of the Roman power. The masters of the Roman world were ironically very insecure and their leadership was often simply insane. A perceptive person could have seen in these things a civilization that was no longer worthy of the name and which was collapsing in on itself. Meanwhile the inner dignity of the nonmilitant martyrs, the women as well as the men, the young as well as the old, won much respect and strengthened the faith of many. As Tertullian, a Christian writer of the time, said, "The blood of the martyrs is *the seed*," the cause or basis of the new faith's growing influence in the slowly crumbling Roman empire.

When the very worst and widest persecution took place, Christians in Rome hid for lengthy periods of time in underground cemetery tunnels called the Catacombs. Then, in the year 311, the emperor Galerius suddenly reversed his own policy and freed the Christian faith from official persecution. Two years later, after his death, an imperial edict made religious tolerance the rule in all the empire's far-flung regions.

During the foregoing two-and-a-half centuries of occasional waves of slaughter, not even one incident of organized armed resistance by Christians was recorded. Their leaders forbade violence, urging believers to pray for their persecutors and to offer no unnecessary offense. No church issued a call for a revolutionary Christian state, whether for a homeland of believers or for a Christianized Roman empire. "Our struggle is not with flesh-and-blood," said their sacred writings, "but against the *spiritual* wickedness of princedoms and powers in high places." The believers had been restrained from physical attacks on their enemies but in their refusal to have their spirits broken by the worst forces of social domination, they had denied the frustrated powers even the illusion of absolute control.

6. The new and the old

Though it can't be said that Christians during these volatile times always had opportunity to learn of their faith in a balanced and accurate form, it certainly appears that the new way had come through the fires of persecution reasonably well. Something essential had taken root: an appreciation of the kingdom of the heart and spirit, as distinct from an earthly reign over territory to be maintained with the sword. As long as the maltreatment continued, believers held to that foundational outlook. That is why Hebrew Christians chose not to make common cause with the more militant factions among their fellow Jews, though Rome's brutality hit them both.

Judaism and Christianity increasingly went their separate ways after the fall of Jerusalem in the year 70. Then, as more and more Gentiles entered the ranks of Christian believers, their main concerns turned away from Jewish questions, away from the relationship between the old and new covenants, and the distinction between law and grace. It became more important to know how the church related to society and state, and how the "catholic" teachings compared with the influences of Classical Pagan civilization. When official tolerance arrived, it is these issues of believers within the larger society that were often the focus of Christian thought and discussion.

So the newer beliefs of the kingdom were surviving the violent trials. With that outcome, it seemed I was only a few steps away of seeing the conclusion of the long epic story. Was the new kingdom then ready to be revealed in more visible form? But how could that be if the spirituality of Abraham as opened up by Yeshua apparently was all but lost over the years? The search was not quite over.

Chapter Thirteen
The quest re-made

1. A change at the top

On the northwestern edge of the empire, icy February rains had been plaguing the Roman fortress of Eboracum in Britain, but the grey skies lay quiet long enough for legionaries to file into their ranks on the soaking turf outside. These soldiers were mostly "Teutsch" or Teutons, men who were conscripted from Germany. With muddied cloaks over their rough woolen tunics, leggings, and leather armor, they stood on the grimy wet ground with their faces in the direction of the settlement that was later known as York. Probably not one of the soldiers so much as heard of the kingdom epic because few Germanic tribes had been in contact with "the People of the Book," but they would find something out about it before very long.

One of their German-born commanders broke the news to them that their leader, the augustus or co-emperor, had died. Inside their cloaks the soldiers shivered. The politics of leadership in the empire was always volatile and troops were of necessity fiercely loyal to any military contender whose success would give them better honor and pay. If their leader was now dead, what would their future be? But their commander had news for them.

The officer turned to face his general, the son of the deceased co-emperor, who stood on a stone platform beside the gate. He raised his arm in salute to him and shouted, "All hail *Constantine*, our new augustus!" The legionaries thundered back their response: "Hail Constantine Augustus!" The general then signaled acceptance of the salute, confident that his army would loyally march with him all the way to Rome if he so chose. It was this act of recognition from his troops that launched the general toward becoming the Roman empire's only sovereign, though it would be a journey of eighteen years to get that far.

Constantine had been born in Serbia to an ambitious Roman general and an innkeeper's daughter. The son eventually became a general in his own right and was serving in Britain to deal with attacks from Pict tribes of Scotland when he received word of his father's passing. His mother Helen was a Christian. He adored her but had been too busy with advancing his career to consider her beliefs carefully. Yet later on, nearing Rome to press his claim to the imperial throne, he superstitiously had his soldiers paint on their shields the Greek letters *chi-rho (XP)*, an abbreviation for the word "Christ." The subsequent battle victory at a shallow river-crossing called Milvian Bridge increased his interest in the despised faith. The very next year, in 313, he urged the other heads of the empire to join him in granting tolerance to all religions.

In due time, the general became the supreme emperor and then took an historically momentous step: he moved the empire's capital from Rome to Byzantium, a great eastern metropolis which was then given the name "City of Constantine" (Constantinople, later shortened to Istanbul by the Turks). It was both a practical step and a bold break with tradition. In the new capital, he was free of "the old guard" and was able to instigate the changes that began a long process of Christianizing the empire.

Christianizing the empire? How could a thing like that be done if the "empire" that Christians were called to serve was a spiritual kingdom? How could the deepest desires of the human heart be channeled into an ambitious imperial program for conquered political units? In the ancient world, at least, it could be tried. Here I stood at the threshold of many revisions to the kingdom, changes that threatened to undo all that the epic had slowly worked up to.

As a former Pagan, the emperor kept some of his old ways of thinking and doing, though he did begin to speak openly of his growing faith, writing letters to church leaders, giving generously for the care of ministers of the gospel and providing for many of the poor. Banning crucifixion, he withdrew royal support for gladiator games, declared Sunday as a day of rest in the cities, and spent large sums to build new meeting places for Christian worshippers. All this was welcomed by Christians everywhere, though the changes in society came not by a transformation of people's hearts and minds as much as by an autocratic political system.

These developments, of course, have to be seen against the background of earlier fierce persecutions by Roman Paganism. Christians thanked God for the unexpected rise of a man like Constantine, but the emperor was prepared to go to considerable lengths to promote a new version of Roman society. When he discovered that Christians had very divisive arguments among themselves, he decided to intervene, calling all church leaders together to end the threat of widespread religious conflict in his domain. It seemed a wise and worthy thing for an emperor to do and yet it was precisely this active interest of Constantine in establishing the religion of his mother that was to present a huge challenge to the new spiritual kingdom. It was a challenge even greater than the trial imposed by the Pagan persecutions.

2. Making change systematic

An increasing number of Greek intellectuals, people highly educated in Classical thought and reasoning, had been converting to Christianity during the centuries between Christ and Constantine. They came up against the fact that much of what was known about Yeshua had an air of mystery to it. Even some non-Christian intellectuals such as Josephus acknowledged that the man of Nazareth had been much more than an ordinary person. It was said that Yeshua was a sort of second Adam, the start and chief representative of a new phase of human life, and this was something the thinkers wanted to develop into a more systematic understanding.

By doing this, some scholars wanted to achieve an intellectually respectable defense for the faith, while some thinkers looked for greater academic rigor in order to counter the views of the Gnostics and others. But it was also just the mental habit of thinkers to try to remove as much mystery as possible. As always among academics, hypotheses and theories were fought over with much gusto and with professional reputations at stake. The mystery of faith became the subject of meticulous study, scholarly jargon and schismatic debate, while each side in the arguments believed its own formulation to be the most correct form of truth, even exclusively so.

During Constantine's time, a major debate of this kind erupted in the Egyptian city of *Alexandria,* the empire's Greek-speaking center of learning — the major university town, we might say today. *Arius,* a leader of the church there, thought that Yeshua had lower status than God the Father because he was human, though apparently also divine. A vocal opponent from the same church, *Athanasius* by name, held rather that "the Father and Jesus Christ the Son of God" are jointly eternal and that their "family" relationship was not to be taken literally. The war of words was on.

Athanasius' opponents charged him with using raw intimidation, saying he had provocateurs that could start a riot in the city on his behalf whenever required. Kidnapping, beatings, jailing, and excommunication (removal of church fellowship) were alleged to be his methods. The charges rarely stuck, but like others in the dispute, Athanasius firmly believed that great consequences were involved. He said, "What is at stake is not just a theological theory but people's salvation." If any of the charges against him were true and not just a tactic of the opposing side, this would be the first major instance of a Christian leader justifying violence and coercion as a way of saving people. In any case, the reconciling and peace-giving aspect of the gospel was starting to be lost amid the fierce debates.

Noting the intensity of the disagreements, Constantine called all churches to a conference in the town of Nicea, not far from the capital city, for the purpose of having Christians set some empire-wide standards of belief and practice. Church leaders came, debated some more, and then voted overwhelmingly against the views of Arius and in favor of Athanasius. The conference also gave direction on other things, including some technical matters of worship (for example, they made a peculiar rule that Easter should not be celebrated at the same time as the Jewish Pass-over, though historically the two had coincided).

Nicea had begun a long tradition of periodic "ecumenical councils" to deal with contentious issues on behalf of most churches. Yet these consultations didn't always lead to harmony and truth, and sometimes a later council would reverse the decision of an earlier one. Seeds of bitterness were sown and Yeshua's main teachings were now in the hands of people having a strong ill-will. Over the years, even the good intentions behind clarifying verdicts on points of theology came to be spoiled by fierce curses called "anathemas" and other attacks on those who held different views.

Unfortunately, this furious style grew to be a common and generally accepted form of discourse in Christianity. The ability to use eloquent language to denounce those who took another approach became thought of as being a sign of strong spirituality. But it was just one indication among others that many followers of Yeshua did "not know of what spirit" they were.

3. Back to domination

In the time between the apostles and the councils, local church overseers called *bishops* had come to be accepted as being *canons* ("canes," authoritative standards of straightness and truth). Sometimes this idea of authority clashed with the power of insight, whether it was the insight of experience, the inner wisdom of the spirit, or the hidden knowledge of the Gnostics. But when bishops assembled at an ecumenical council, their conclusions were intended to be binding on all, regardless of personal persuasions. The increasing number of decisions by the bishops therefore started growing into a new body of *religious law*.

Few people of those days seem to have had difficulty

reconciling this renewed interest in religious law with one of the most basic ideas of the new kingdom and covenant, that of individual freedom from many religious statutes and traditions of behavior. And because so few believers noticed the discrepancy, it became easier for anyone who insisted on that freedom to be suspected of being a rebel and a heretic.

One particularly ominous aspect of the first council at Nicea was the special designation it gave to the churches at Rome and Alexandria. These two centers were allowed a status of being first-among-equals in their own geographical regions, though the Constantinople church also wanted special status, as did the church of Antioch in Syria, both claiming that such privilege had been conferred on them by the emperor. Down to the present day, there have been four separate Christian denominations based in those four cities: the Coptic Church (of Alexandria), the Antiochan Orthodox (Syrian Antioch is now located in Turkey), the Greek Orthodox (no longer based in the now Muslim city of Istanbul but having a large following in some Slavic nations), and the largest church, the Roman Catholic in the empire's old capital. Undoubtedly, this long-lasting interest in rank was yet another departure from the spiritual kingdom.

The Syrian church dismissed all those of their members who thought that Yeshua the Messiah had "one nature" (the divine in a human form) because that was against the official view of "two natures" (fully divine and fully human). Many in the ousted group, known after its leader's name as *Nestorians*, left the area and moved further east, becoming numerous in Iran and settling at many places along the caravan routes to the far orient (where Marco Polo discovered them alive and well centuries later, even in the courts of emperor Kublai Khan in China).

The Coptic Church held to a middle view, namely that though Yeshua had two natures, these two were united into one. When one of the ecumenical councils heard of this, the entire Egyptian church was denounced. Such hair-splitting, highly dubious reasons for turning against friends of the faith can only make some sense in an authoritarian system in which there is an express desire to dominate. Perhaps the real reason for the harshness was that the Coptic Church had its separate regional traditions and even its own pope!

Meanwhile, there were other changes affecting the faith. With money from the emperor, the newly ornate church buildings developed worship into a matter of elaborate ritual. An ordinary wooden table that had usually been the centerpiece for commemorating the last supper of Christ was gradually being replaced by a fancy altar, the focus of a ritual that re-introduced into Christianity the notion of ongoing sacrifices (the repeated sacrifice of Christ's body). This altar then became off-limits to ordinary members of the congregation.

Likewise, the clothes of the nobility, their fancy robes and head-gear, became the uniform of church leaders as they were now set apart from their people to be a special social class of ministers. The commonly-used Greek root-word *presbyter,* which in Christianity's earliest days had simply meant "elder" (the general title of a leader in a spiritual community), in due time was shortened to *prester* and then became *priester* or (in English) *priest,* to signify a member of an exclusive and certified religious rank.

Many Christians, to be sure, rejoiced in this growing church bureaucracy, proud of a glorious holy kingdom that looked increasingly like other kingdoms on Earth, all within a grand empire headed by Christian caesars. But there were other believers who shook their heads at these developments and looked in a very different direction for evidence of the kingdom of God.

4. *The individual retreats*

In out-of-the-way places, far from civilization's institutions, wealth, and daily complications, lived "the desert fathers" (and mothers) who had entered on a solitary life devoted to gaining the peace of inner light. They resided in caves or grass huts, battling their own demons, memories, depression and fears. Even in their quiet way, these hermits lived an extreme and hazardous existence, and not all who began this life came out with a balanced mind. Nevertheless, in time some became known in their localities as wise and holy persons whose words and insights were simple but profound.

One of the most famous of these seekers was a man called *Anthony* (Antony). While he pioneered some of the severe habits of the pious hermit, he also went into the village to kindly minister to ordinary folks. Conscious that there had to be a balance, he gathered other seekers around him, each in his own cell but not far away, forming a community of monks. But though Anthony believed in human contact, he held that solitary contemplation should always come first. He said,

> Just as fish die if they stay out of water too long, so monks who loiter outside their cells or pass time with men of the world lose the fervor of inner peace. So, like a fish going toward the sea, we must hurry to reach our cell, for fear that if we tarry outside we will lose our interior watchfulness.

It was to be expected that the common people came to regard these dedicated men and women with a mixture of curiosity and awe. As the social and material status of clergy in the cities improved, the contrasting self-denial of the desert dwellers (primarily in Egypt and spreading from there to other places) was celebrated. So much were the hermits esteemed that there was now a growing danger that "the holy life" would become redefined as the lifestyle of monks and nuns.

While there were still some preachers who went against both trends, against both the wealthy establishment and the poverty-stricken hermitage, the years of peace became more than simply a blessed relief from persecution. They were also a perilous trap for Christians' faith and life. As the ordinary occupations of believers started to be seen as inferior, unworthy of special blessing, there seemed little hope that the working family person could be spiritual. Moreover, the desert hermits showed too little appreciation of the goodness of nature, of how important the divine invasion of living things was to Earth and those who inherit it.

5. Springing the trap

The perilous trap had been set, not only by sincere monks and nuns but especially by well-meaning but mistaken leaders of both church and state. The trap was really sprung when the many changes brought by Constantine were extended and increased by a team of two later emperors, *Gratian* in the west and *Theodosius* in the east. Acting together, they brought imperial law to bear heavily on spiritual matters. Going a step beyond Constantine, the two made it a legal requirement that everyone in the empire must accept the Nicea version of the Christian faith. Here is the stern text of that legislation:

> We authorize the followers of this law to assume the title of *Catholic Christians;* but as for the others, since, in our judgment they are foolish madmen, we decree that they shall be branded with the ignominious name of *heretics,* and shall not presume to give to their conventicles the name of churches. They will suffer in the first place the chastisement of the divine condemnation and in the second the punishment of our authority which in accordance with the will of Heaven we shall decide to inflict.

How ironic that was: the spiritual mission of a humble Galilean revised to become the official state religion, and the Nicene Creed its exclusive theology by force of law! When the empire was constitutionally made Christian and Nicene, a new reality appeared in the world, something that came to be called *Christendom,* the "Christian domain." Christendom in this sense means the territory that is formally Christian and whose culture has to some degree been shaped by the dominant version of Christianity. The faith was becoming a political and cultural expression and only secondarily a matter of the heart and spirit.

6. *Quiet as yeast*

It looked as if there would be no happy ending to the epic. The uneasy alliance of church and state had captured and hijacked the outcome of the long story, bringing back the idea of a political kingdom of God. But then something happened that revealed an uncannily quiet power, invisible to the emperor though moving almost within his shadow.

At the emperor's court worked a high official by the name of *Pontitianus,* a Roman citizen from northern Africa. One day, Ponty (as we'll call him) happened to visit a couple of younger acquaintances, one of whom was a fellow African, a perennial student called *Augustine.* Seeing that Augustine was reading a copy of one of Paul's letters, Ponty told him what happened recently when he had gone for a walk with another government agent.

The story was that Ponty and his co-worker had come across a cottage where they entered into a friendly discussion with the resident. The cottager showed them a little book on the life of the hermit Anthony and they all sat down as the man read to them from the book. What happened during the reading was carefully documented by Augustine the way he heard it from Ponty:

> Pontitianus looked at the co-worker and said, "So, tell me what we are achieving with all our work? What is our aim and why do we serve? Can our hopes at the court rise higher than being the emperor's favorites — a fragile thing, full of peril? How many of these perils do we have to have just so we can arrive at a greater one?
>
> ...He turned his eyes to the man's book and read on, changing inwardly. For as he read and turned the pages of his heart, he railed against

himself a while but then found a better response. He said to his friend, "Now I've broken loose from these hopes of ours and am resolved to serve God. I start now in this hour, in this place..." So they both began, having counted the cost. Forsaking everything, they followed God.

Ponty too had become a sojourner instead of the social climber he had been. He left Augustine and his friend, not knowing what effect his personal account would have on the young men. Augustine was an earnest and already accomplished scholar, much engaged in the pursuit of wisdom but also much in love with pleasure. In a wretched moment, he had begged God for relief from his very active sex drive — well, sort of: "Give me chastity and continence, only not yet." But his wide-ranging studies had brought him a certain amount of humility about his own views and Ponty's story had now suddenly increased that.

"What's wrong with us?" Augustine exclaimed, turning to his friend. "The unlearned get up and take heaven by storm while we, with our education and without heart, wallow in flesh and blood! Are we ashamed to follow them because we didn't think of it ourselves?"

In agony of spirit, Augustine left his friend for a short while to walk in an adjoining garden. As he wept and spoke to himself, he heard the voice of a child in a neighboring house, chanting, "Take up and read, take up and read." The words took hold of him. Were there any children's games that had these words in a song? He couldn't think of any. Quieting his feelings, Augustine accepted the child's voice as a message from God.

Quickly, he returned to his friend and picked up the letter of Paul that he had been reading earlier. His eyes then fell on this sentence: "...not in partying and drunkenness, not in bed-hopping and excesses, not in strife and jealousy — but put on (the spirit of) the Lord Jesus Christ and make no plans to satisfy the lusts of the flesh." Somehow these words, at that moment, gave him strength and quieted his heart. Augustine was at last ready for a great turning point in his life.

A strange act of spirit and word had brought about a sudden and deep inner change in the ambitious Ponty and his worldly-successful co-worker, and it now did the same for the academic Augustine and his companion. We know of these four converts of the heart because they didn't drop out of society by going to the desert but stayed in circulation and had their story published. Augustine went on to become one of the most influential people in the history of the west and wrote the account which we have quoted. We understand, however, that there were many others whose names and stories were never made public outside of their immediate circles, yet who also were changed in a similar manner.

History books make little of these intense personal transformations and instead focus on the acts of emperors and bishops and on the development of social powers, but there was something powerful afoot that could not easily be analyzed, something that had started to change the times in a much less visible way. It was because of such developments in the general population, among ordinary people and not just a chosen few, that the world and the human race could never really be quite the same again. Ponty had led his friends over a bridge out of the ancient world. While state and church made laws and took the credit for progress, unexpected transformations were happening to people one or two at a time, and such people did not feel deeply indebted to social institutions.

Individual spiritual change was on the move, almost invisibly, within a world of loud social domination and many backward-looking changes that had been affecting all Abrahamic believers. The quiet movement rarely opposed that domination and deterioration directly, but rather went on its own way in a very different direction. How like Abraham that was! His old promise now had its greatest hope of being fulfilled, and the long span of the ancient era could finally draw to a close.

A Kingdom for the Heart

A timely retelling of an ancient epic

The new setting

Chapter Fourteen
The world after the epic

1. The rest of the forest

We now have seen the close of the ancient era, and it ended not with a solid conclusion but with a set of possibilities. Abraham's spiritual quest had finally begun to spread to the world as increasing numbers of people in many countries found a way into a security and personal hope beyond land or law. This access was direct, available to anyone, and not needing the structured involvement of instituted religion or the agendas of a dominating state. Neither could pious exercises or techniques much enhance the inner strength.

Not all my questions had found satisfactory answers. There was still this problem of severe inconsistency in those who claimed to be citizens of the spiritual kingdom. I realized that in part this was just common, unsolvable human weakness, as well as immaturity and lack of adequate inner development. It could be forgiven and set aside as being of secondary importance as long as the inconsistency did not intend to quash the new spirituality. At least there was, at the end of the ancient age, a sense that a certain presence and motivation was being felt in the world, beyond religious doctrine and custom. Many ordinary people were sensing this, quite apart from the impressions made on them by evangelistic or mystical techniques.

Soon the ancient era would also end for nations outside of the Roman empire. Less than two centuries after Augustine, Arabs would start to divide their own history into a dim past and a brighter present. I've saved their story for this final chapter rather than include it as part of the epic itself because it properly belongs to the period of time that follows the ancient age and that deals with the problem of what to do about errors within Judaism and Christianity. It is important to have Islam in the closing part of this book as one of the three major families of Abraham.

In any event, for all of us of the present century, the epic is long since over. Maybe the best way to put it is that we are living in the *sequel,* still feeling the influence of that old story. Even after all these years, we can still see some of the epic's importance in today's news headlines, in the endless conflicts in the Middle East, from Turkey to Arabia to Afghanistan and everywhere in between. These ongoing tragedies involve nations that invoke the name of Abraham, where his story is heard in garbled form among the noises of argument and battle, both political and religious.

Our consideration of the origins of Islam at the end of the ancient days will also bring a brief introduction to the medieval and modern eras. That will allow a short overview of how all the children of Abraham have dealt with the challenge of a kingdom for the heart. Here then, like a movie preview, is a glance at the sequel, at what the rest of "the forest" looks like.

2. The crescent moon rises

The dimmer light of the crescent moon and the night star can be more welcome in the subtropical desert than the flaming glare of the daytime sun, and in the land of deserts the ancient age ended about two hundred years after Augustine with a set of earth-shaking religious events. Rather than be overtaken by the older Abrahamic faiths, tribes in the Arabian wilderness submitted themselves to a native revision of these and thus a new era began.

In the year 610, the Arab merchant Muhammad began receiving revelations that continued on until his death in 632. These messages from the angel Gabriel included frequent dire warnings to pay them attention, as well as calls to remember God's mercy. They contained instructions for life and worship with repeated illustrations from the lives of Adam, Abraham and the biblical Hebrews.

Muhammad's revelations fit well into his stark, sandy environment. Reading his writings, we can imagine that we are in Arabia or else back at Mount Horeb in the Sinai desert, moved by the fear of God and the sacred law. His was a strong message against trespasses, meant to be strongly received.

> These are the limits Allah has set. Whoever obeys Allah and his messenger will be allowed to enter gardens where rivers flow, where one can reside forever. That will be the great outcome. But whoever disobeys Allah and his messenger and breaks his limits, will be made to enter the place of fire, where one will reside forever. That will be a disgraceful destiny.

In the year 622, after Muhammad and his followers were persecuted in his hometown of Mecca (Makkah), they fled north to the city of Yathrib (later renamed Al-Madinah or Medina). He made a pact of peace among the clans living there, including a large number of Jews. According to the agreement, Jews would enjoy equal rights with his followers so long as they supported the pact. In due time, the Prophet announced that he had received a revelation to meet persecution with force, and without much delay he attacked a Mecca caravan returning from trade in Syria. After further military gains and losses, Muhammad left Medina and took over the crucial city of Mecca.

From the renewed base in Arabia's most important population center, the Prophet worked hard to benefit the fragmented, polytheistic and superstitious Arab tribes by banning idolatry and imposing the regulated worship of the one God. His new religion became known as *Islam,* a word that refers to "submission" to Abraham's God, who is called *Allah* in Arabic, much like the Hebrew *Eloh* (both are Semitic languages). At first, Muhammad faced Jerusalem when offering daily prayers but when some of the Medina Jews turned against him, he was so stung by what he regarded as a treasonous breaking of his pact with them that he consented to have them put to death. After this pivotal event, he received a revelation to turn his face away from Jerusalem and from then on to face Mecca whenever he prayed.

Muhammad viewed his revelations as correcting the shortcomings or misinterpretations of the Hebrew and Christian religions. As we saw in the epic, there certainly was a need for correction. The more reform-minded people among the Jews and Christians had their own ideas of what to do with huge inconsistencies of belief and behavior within their communities, but Muhammad considered himself to be the last word, God's final messenger in a long line of biblical prophets. He was the Prophet for this age, sent by Allah to the Arab descendants of Ishmael.

After Muhammad's death, his written revelations were assembled into one holy book known as the *Qur'an* (*Koran*). Muslims believe that the Qur'an is a "recitation" from God and that it is so potent in the Arab language that the mere reading or hearing of it gives life and power, even aside from submission to its teachings. Unlike the epic of the kingdom in general, the Muslim holy book doesn't read like a developing story but rather is a set of final revelations that preach and teach, with brief illustrations involving some biblical people. Its main focus is on the doctrine and law of Allah.

For many Muslim scholars the Prophet has especially been "The Lawgiver," whose life and knowledge form the basis of all Islamic law. That legal focus was enlarged and codified over the centuries into *sharia*, the law code that covers all aspects of life from the personal daily practices of believers to the public duties of Islamic societies. The number of legal requirements for Muslims was small, five main ones ("the Pillars") plus some strict laws of diet and form, but the way Islam continued to develop after the Prophet's time certainly had its parallels in the experience of Jews and Christians, as rules and customs multiplied. Law-mindedness also expressed itself in divisions over the issue of his legally-correct successor. The disagreement brought bloodshed, permanently splitting the Islamic world into the major factions known as *Sunni* and *Shia,* and later into many further Shia divisions based on the same question ("Who is the rightful Caliph or Imam?").

Muhammad had been both Prophet and Ruler of Arabia, and so there was always a close tie between the faith and the land. Islam's physical boundaries were expanded through military conquests, bringing Islamic law to Africa and Spain, Palestine and Syria, Mesopotamia and Persia, Turkey and eastern Europe. Thereby the connection between faith and land was strengthened over a sizeable portion of the world. The invasions multiplied Islam's major shrines, going beyond the holy cities in Arabia to now include Jerusalem and a number of special mosques in Iraq and Iran (which is one significant reason why Muslims think these lands must never be controlled by westerners).

Islam had been new to the Arabs and yet it in some ways it represented a return to an earlier era in the larger world, to a time before Yeshua and Paul. But for the desert societies of Muhammad's time, steeped in loosely-related sets of customs and superstitions, the introduction of the law of Allah did bring change for the better, since Islam's significant benefit to the Arab tribes of that day is hardly debatable. Moreover, the new territories of the Arabs produced culturally rich societies, built on the older Christian and Classical traditions of most of these lands. Islamic civilization borrowed from the older societies and added its own framework until it rivaled and surpassed ancient Persia, imperial Rome and early Christian Europe.

In addition to Muslim learning, arts, medicine, architecture, and other features, the new civilization was superior in the way it treated people of different faith (at least it was so in the early centuries), even within the context of holy war. Therefore not all Christians saw the change of power in their homelands as a tragedy and some actually welcomed the Muslim invaders as liberators. Though forced to live as second-class members of society, Christians in Islamic lands were generally treated with greater tolerance than what they had gotten from fellow believers who had differed in some theological opinions. Islam brought a measure of relief for those who had been condemned by bishop or emperor as being heretics.

A member of Syria's Nestorian church of those times wrote: "The hearts of Christians rejoiced at the domination of the Arabs; may God strengthen it and prosper it." Another said, "the God of vengeance has raised the children of Ishmael to deliver us by them from the hands of the Romans." The Coptic Christians of Egypt were also treated well as long as they paid a special tax, and one of Muhammad's wives was a Copt named Mary. In time, tolerance would break down and in various lands severe restrictions or even death would be enforced as punishment for not being Muslim, but to the underdog the news of conquest was welcome at first. Though not seeming to understand the message of the spiritual kingdom very well, Islam certainly was a rebuke to many who thought they were Yeshua's followers.

For six centuries, Islamic civilization grew and flourished. Then it entered a long period of decline brought about by many internal divisions, much religious formality, the Crusades, and especially by repeated devastations at the hand of the Mongols, an almost genocidal Asiatic nation bent on destroying urban civilization. By the year 1400, a large part of the Islamic world had suffered attack and destruction, most notably the religiously and culturally significant land of Iraq. Muslims struggled with the thought that this loss of success seemed to mean a loss of divine favor.

The downturn now made room for new approaches in Islam, such as the *Sufi* variety which was focused on feelings and experiences. The Sufi sects had no single set of theological doctrines, although they tended to say that God manifests himself in his people, either in all humans or in the mystical experiences of some, or even in nature generally. This transcendental outlook of the Sufis sounded like pure heresy to conventional Muslims. In Baghdad and some other places, Sufis were persecuted, and one of their teachers was scourged and crucified to imitate the death of Isa/Yeshua who also had claimed to manifest God. Though a few Sufis were very unreligious in their practice, seeing little spiritual benefit in Islamic law, they generally used meditation on the Qur'an as a way of trying to purify the soul, adding that discipline to their habit of religious singing and dancing.

Overall decline in Islam also led to efforts at restoring the old ways. In the 1700s, an Arabic reform movement grew from the teachings of Muhammad al-Wahab who wanted to purge Islam of everything that was not exactly the tradition of the religion's earliest centuries. To this puritanical view he converted the Saudi family and their tribe, who came to control most of Arabia. This conservative *Wahabi* movement has since inspired a large number of reform-minded Islamists, but it became especially known for some groups within it that advocated violence as a means to advance the cause of a purer Islam. In the present situation that includes the terrorist network called *al-Qaeda*.

In the twentieth century, large numbers of Muslims emigrated to the West. There, outside of Islamic society, they were faced with the considerable challenge of following their religion without the regulation and support of an entire community. They also became more familiar with the way that modern nations were trying to solve their conflicts through international law and conferences rather than through holy war. In fact, because there now were these peaceful options, the warlike version of *jihad* came to be viewed by many Muslims as no longer required or legal. And the second generation, more westernized than the original immigrants, did not necessarily want to abide by all the traditions anyway. The question that faced them was this: "Can our Abrahamic faith become a personal strength that does not need to be vigorously enforced by family and holy law, by mullah and state?" Undoubtedly, this will remain an issue for many years to come,

3. The Chosen People without a home

There have been close parallels in the experience of Muslim and Jew, which we can see as we turn to the Hebrew story of the time after the ancient days. With the destruction of Jerusalem and its temple in the year 70, the long centralization of Hebrew faith ended. Jews could no longer travel to Jerusalem to worship in the grand old manner, and their population continued to spread out over the world. They became wanderers like their ancestors Abraham and Jacob, and their many local meeting halls called synagogues became the heart of religious activity. There, discussions of the spoken Hebrew traditions were organized, leading in time to a standard collection of the oral law, called the *Mishnah*. Other leaders worked on various law commentaries (*Talmud*) over the next few centuries.

With the majority of Jews no longer living in the "Eretz Yisrael," the promised land of Israel, the land-based kingdom could no longer be their daily concern, and the temple's destruction ended all its sacrifices and related rituals. The synagogues did not take over the temple's function of making blood offerings, and by implication there was no regular atonement for the sins of the people anymore. The whole matter of being God's chosen people now had to focus on something other than the priestly worship and sacrifices, and it also had to involve something different from the political agitation which had proved so horribly disastrous.

That "something" was the religious teaching in the family home, as confirmed by the synagogue where the law in all its detail for common daily life was read and expounded. The teaching of the religious law and the making of studious commentaries on it, continued to be a major task of synagogue rabbis for many centuries, right into the Middle Ages. Among these numerous efforts was the work of *Rabbi Moses ben Maimon* (affectionately known by the abbreviation "Rambam") who arranged the many written and oral traditions into one huge code of law.

From the time of the Middle Ages, there evolved two main types of Judaism: the conservative *Ashkenazi* type, originating in central Europe, and the more cultured or liberal *Sephardic* kind, coming out of Spain and spreading far to the east. Spanish king Ferdinand and his queen Isabella expelled all Jews from their land in the year 1492 (when they also let Columbus sail the ocean blue), amid upheavals and persecutions in various other countries. The chaos of these times and the forced travels of Jews now began to make possible the spread of the less-orthodox types of Judaism. An interest in numerology and in symbolic interpretations of the law started to receive a hearing, as did philosophical speculations about God and the creation. Many of these ideas were said to be based on secret teachings handed down by small elite groups, not unlike those Gnostic secret societies of earlier Christian times. Collectively, the more mystic views in Judaism, when written down, became known as the *Cabala (Qabbala)*.

The modern era brought new kinds of developments. In the eighteenth century, two entirely different approaches to Jewish spirituality were taken by the *Hasidic* and *Haskalah* movements. To get a flavor of these and their effect on Judaism, think of the religious issues and styles in the Broadway musical and film production of *The Fiddler on the Roof*, though the setting of that play is over a century later. Hasidic Jews, mostly in eastern Europe, reacted against the rigidly law-centered, formal religion of their place and time. Instead, in their own Yiddish language they emphasized personal piety and a worshipful joy, with music and even dance. Here was some greater attention to the happiness and empowerment of the common people, even though they stood in awe of their leaders who were called *rebbi* (teacher) or *zadik* (righteous one). While this Hasidism was strongly opposed by many rabbis in more traditional synagogues, the movement spread across eastern Europe, from Poland to the Ukraine.

The special piety of Hasidism was practiced mostly within the ghetto, the Yiddish-speaking Jewish quarter of various European cities. The Haskalah party, on the other hand, urged Jews to break out of the ghetto and get more involved with European civilization. Haskalah's best example of their "Jewish Enlightenment" movement was *Moses Mendelssohn,* who translated the Bible into German, urging people to go beyond the usual applications that the rabbis taught. Through the German Bible, he hoped they would learn to know what the text actually meant, and replace the rabbinic teachings with the Scriptures' larger spiritual and relational principles. His views bore a similarity to those of the great Hillel (an esteemed teacher just before the time of Yeshua), and they were not unlike the words of Yeshua himself.

As Jews became familiar with Mendelssohn's Bible, they used its language to open doors to German society as a whole. An unintended outcome of this openness, and of the Haskalah movement generally, was that many Jews left Judaism to join liberally-minded churches in which Christian and Jew could both shake off traditional restrictions. Yet, in those days there was no real social equality outside of the established state church, not even for Christians of other churches, and Jews who liberated themselves from the ghetto soon found out that it took more than language and education, or even baptism, to find full acceptance.

Society's lack of respect would occasionally motivate a Hebrew leader to take a group of hurt but hopeful immigrants back to the Eretz Yisrael. During the 1700s, a substantial number of Jews settled in Galilee, expecting that the Messiah would soon appear. The longing for the Holy Land grew stronger in the nineteenth century when persecutions became more intense. Then a man called *Theodor Hertzl,* after watching anti-Semitism spread from the law courts of France to mobs in the streets of Paris and other cities, began to promote "Zionism." This was a belief that Jews could never fulfill their personal and ethnic destinies outside of a homeland, a country of their own. Although Hertzl at first had other locations in mind, for most Jews such a place of home could be none other than the Holy Land.

After the First World War, the British gained control of

Palestine and initially supported the establishment of the Jewish "national home." Following the unprecedented systematic horror of *ha-Shoah*, the Holocaust in which six million Jews died at the hands of Nazis in World War Two, the United Nations accepted the creation of an independent Jewish state within the borders of Palestine. That decision, however, did not suit a new militant nationalism that was rising at this same time among Arabs and Palestinians. Even among Jews, the modern state of Israel did not receive absolute favor. A few pointed out that the state was founded without a clear reference to Messiah's kingdom. Some were also troubled by a similarity to the ancient Hasmonean and Zealot policies, especially because the new state needed to use frequent military force to protect itself from its hostile neighbors.

Aside from a large immigration to Israel following the Second World War, Jews in the West often preferred to stay where they already lived, especially in the United States which had a larger Jewish population than any other nation, including Israel. Many American Jews continued to assimilate with the general culture, observing the holy laws and feast days less religiously and less often. "Jewishness" came to be more about individual belief and preference and less about a religious identity or a strictly ethnic one. This was somewhat of a parallel to the spiritual kingdom.

4. The Christian difficulty

Lastly, let's catch a glimpse of how the uniqueness of Yeshua's teachings fared within Christianity, for the whole history of that religion illustrates the difficulty their people have had in understanding the marks of the spiritual kingdom. From the beginning, the question was debated of how different the world of the heart and spirit was from the old religious law. This had been a major Christian theme, especially in the New Testament, and from time to time the thorny question found new people willing to ponder it.

Christian missions to Pagan Europe reflected the difficulty

in a particularly interesting way. After Islam took over much of southern and eastern Christendom, Christians looked to the more northern parts of Europe as an area where the faith might be spread, and a number of earlier efforts had already been made in that direction. One of the common practices among preachers of the gospel was to start with a tribal leader, knowing that he controlled the religion of all his people. When the leader was baptized, often the whole tribe was as well, becoming Christian in name but not necessarily in heart and mind. Eventually some of these people would be appointed as priests, dubiously converted and poorly trained.

Similarly, famous Frankish emperor Charlemagne fought the fierce Asiatic tribe of the Huns with the intent to convert them to Christianity. After his enemy was defeated in battle, he sent his bishop Arno to have them baptized en masse under military pressure. Of course, as soon as this kind of pressure was removed, the Huns violently renounced their "Christianity." Yet there also were voices speaking out for a more personal and genuine spirituality, such as bishop Alcuin of York, who pointedly asked Charlemagne and Arno, "Of what use is the tongue of a preacher if divine grace has not penetrated the hearts of the hearers?" In such a way the free and spiritual concept of the kingdom of God continued its struggle with the dominating and political one.

In some places the practice of "cross-signing," a kind of half-way baptism, was tried. The English king Athelstan, who was a Christian, required two Norse soldiers of fortune to receive the sign of the cross, presumably a mark made by a priest on a person's forehead. According to one Icelandic saga, "that was a common custom then among both merchants and mercenaries who dealt with Christians; anyone who had taken the sign of the cross could mix freely with both Christians and heathens, while keeping the faith they pleased." For practical reasons, therefore, Pagans in northwestern Europe were not always pressured to convert.

The overall picture is varied and complex. Not all missionaries were agents of Rome, and many originated from the eastern churches or from the Irish-Celtic brand of Christianity, in touch with nature as well as with the spirit. Besides these, there were individuals in Europe who simply went out on their own to preach, teach, and build. Gradually, however, a policy of control by the church hierarchy spread over much of the continent, and Rome began to enforce its authority quite strictly as its interpretations became accepted as being God's will.

Only after many years of being conditioned by a Christian authoritarian system could Europe go along with something like the Crusades. When fiercely-Islamic Turkish tribes from the northeast invaded lands near the Mediterranean Sea and captured the Holy Land with its many shrines and sacred sites, Roman popes called for armed force to turn Palestine into a Christian state. "God wills it!" was the cry, but the Crusades, popular in the romantic imagination of the West, were one of history's most tragically misguided interpretations (or simple disregard) of Yeshua's teachings.

Many Crusaders came from the "Holy Roman Empire." This area of land, covering all of central Europe, was largely a German creation with German emperors who were elected by groups of German kings and nobles. Their participation in crusades called by Italian popes arose from various personal and political motives that somehow straddled a major power struggle between pope and emperor. As a well-known Roman Catholic writer later admitted, the competition here was between "two World States: the Catholic Church and the Holy Roman Empire." The common international goal of these powers: to control Europe and the region of the Holy Land.

Still, the Middle Ages in Europe were not the Dark Ages. From the lowest serf to the highest princes there was a creative mix of traditions, Christian, tribal Pagan, and Classical. It was a time of great exertions in engineering and the arts, as well as in spirituality and thought. But all positive developments were quite overshadowed during the 1300s when Christendom began to fail in a major way. The huge epidemic of bubonic plague known as "The Black Death" swept through Europe in a time that was already disastrous because of famine, war, and the introduction of canon fire. Millions died and thousands of villages and towns were left deserted. It certainly felt as if the end of the world was at hand and that Christendom was being judged. The church found little that was useful or comforting to say in the midst of this unmatched disaster when at least one-third of all Europeans died within the space of just three-and-half years.

Amid the wreckage of Europe and the failure of church leadership, people began to turn to new ideas. There arose a fresh concern for ordinary human life and an appreciation of nature. Experiments were made with new lifestyles and with a personal spirituality for common people. Also humanism, the study and exaltation of the human being, became the main style in some places, especially in northern Italy where it developed into the movement we know as *the Renaissance.* And during the fifteenth and sixteenth centuries, insistent calls for the reform of society and religion came from Bohemia (John Hus), Holland (Erasmus of Rotterdam), Germany (Martin Luther), and from Switzerland (Ulrich Zwingli and John Calvin).

With the emergence of the movement for change that came to be known as *the Protestant Reformation,* there appeared in northern and central Europe a wide swirl of protest that was focused on the Bible and keenly opposed to the Catholic hierarchy. The ancient Hebrew and Greek Scriptures were soon being translated into the common languages of the people, opening their eyes to other ways of understanding their faith and world than what they had been taught. There was long and loud opposition to the special powers of priests and bishops, and instead people were being informed of the figurative "priesthood of all believers," the gospel's empowerment of ordinary people, with special authority residing in the Scriptures alone.

Western Christendom was now fracturing amid many doubts aimed at the old church. With less unity came more conflict and war as Christians fought each other bitterly and savagely. The *Anabaptists,* by the standards of the time the most radical and modern of the reforming groups, were cruelly hated by both Catholics and Protestants, though the key Anabaptist belief in the strong separation of church and state was gradually adopted by western society. Over the course of five centuries, Protestantism and Anabaptism inspired a belief in the necessity of personal faith, with implications for the dignity of the common people, improvement of their lot, freedom of religion, of speech and assembly, and the need for much less hierarchy in church and state.

Yet it was a slowly growing awareness. The Reformation got caught up in the new *nationalism* that was sweeping Europe at the same time, resulting in overly-ethnic churches and schools. Over the years, problems were often dealt with by inflicting *legalism* on the congregations, the "Rule of many rules," and the old covenant law remained in a place of honor as preachers struggled to say why.

The Reformation's partial and unfinished improvements were always becoming formal and binding, and that in turn led to one wave of renewal after another as Protestant movements called for further religious reforms or for greater spirituality and social compassion. These movements, from the eighteenth century on, included Evangelicals, Pietists, Utopian Socialists, the Oxford Movement (that inspired the Twelve-Step Groups), and the Holiness Movement (that led to the Salvation Army on the one hand and the Pentecostals on the other). All this activity of renewal was no doubt stirring to many hearts, though it also "stirred the pot" to raise much hostility from both inside and outside of Protestant society.

A controversial movement in the early decades of the twentieth century was the *Social Gospel*. The more radical Social Gospelers were critical of the New Testament and liked to think that the apostle Paul had ruined a revolutionary agenda of Jesus by replacing zealous social change with individual salvation. These radicals, in effect, returned to the ancient belief in a visible earthly kingdom of God, though theirs was more international, democratic, and less violent than the old belief had tended to be. But others in the Social Gospel movement simply saw in both Jesus and Paul a call to work compassionately for the common good, involving both economic and personal aspects.

Christianity had taken on an extremely varied character. In the long run, this great diversity had the overall benefit of paving the way for *pluralism* — the belief in a community where matters of heart and mind are neither imposed nor opposed by threat of force. Pluralistic society was intended to be a place in which people could compete in ideas and products without killing each other, and where they could prosper individually while acknowledging the rights of the disadvantaged and of all others.

Afterword

Looking back now, I see that my early decision to consider the ancient documents as part of one epic was the key toward the findings. That assumption allowed me to press on with the long search until some pieces began to fall into place, and to go even further when there were still loose ends to be tied up. The search was also a discipline to prevent me from dwelling on my own spiritual experience and beliefs. Investigation and not indoctrination was the main aim, and seekers like me, rather than knowers, were my chosen audience.

The great span of years covering the epic and its sequel, in all their phases and developments, has contributed to confusion over what the faith and spirituality of Abraham is. That confusion often leads to a disillusion with the Abrahamic religions, cultures and believers of many places. But disillusion with these things and persons need not turn us into disillusioned people, for one of the great implications of the epic story is that there is something unseen but powerfully active and good at work in the world. Even amid much pain and bewilderment, the universe is unfolding as it should.

As the research continued and discoveries were being made, I knew that what was so increasingly clear and helpful to me would not meet with everyone's acceptance. But no matter. A maturing spirituality, as the epic showed, did not consist of intellectual agreement or feelings of superiority. Instead, it involved a growing appreciation of the High Power and all created life, a love of goodness and freedom, a willingness to bear with pain and delay, and especially an emerging capacity for practical love in balanced, merciful relationships.

The epic also provided its own best defense against those who claim that most of its documents were the product of religious hierarchies intent on promoting their own power. If that was so, the documents did a remarkably poor job of it, for they criticized power structures and those in it, increasingly put the emphasis on the ordinary individual person, and provided a long-range outlook that minimized any glory the powerful might have claimed. Throughout history, people have turned to these sources to find inspiration for change, while those in power have tended to discourage people's right of interpretation or even access to those same sources.

I gather from the epic that maybe spirituality on this planet has to first involve people in some religious practices as a way of learning to be connected to more than worldly dreams and techniques. And perhaps some amount of religious law is needed for those who have a tendency to be unbalanced or overly mystic. The ongoing problem, however, is that those same aids and rituals also hold people back from going much further toward spiritual maturity.

With these things in mind, I now close this journey and project with a marvelous parable from the documents. It sums up the alternative vision and life that is the kingdom for the heart. This meaningful anecdote, with its clear voice expressing what mature spirituality is like, has become one of my beloved short pieces of literature. Perhaps it will be one of the reader's favorites as well.

> There was a wise king who called several of his subjects together. Then he said to them, "When I was hungry you fed me and when I was thirsty you gave me drink. When I was a stranger you showed me hospitality, when I was naked you clothed me, and when I was in prison you visited me."
>
> Astounded at these words, the people answered, "My lord, when did we see you hungry so that we could have fed you, or thirsty and given you drink? You were no stranger among

us so that we should help you, we never saw you in poverty in order to clothe you, nor was there a need to visit you in any prison. So when did we do such things for you?"

Then the king replied, "You are surprised but believe me, when you did these deeds for the least of my citizen brothers, you did them for me. Come, inherit the kingdom prepared for you since the creation of the world."

Next, the king called together another group of his subjects and said to them, "When I was hungry you gave me nothing to eat and when thirsty you gave me no drink. I was a stranger but you did not invite me. When I was naked you gossiped and did not clothe me, when I was weak you judged rather than helped, and when they condemned me to prison, you blamed me for my misfortune and did not visit."

These people, some of whom were attractively-robed and had long been in the king's court, were confounded by the king's words. "But my lord," they objected, "when did we ever see you hungry or thirsty, as a stranger or in poverty, in weakness or in prison, so that we could have failed to minister to your needs?"

And the king replied, "You are surprised but believe me, whatever you did not do for one of the least of my citizen brothers, you did not do it for me."

Then these subjects were punished for their cold hearts, but the others received the inheritance.

Notes

The Abrahamic documents

Quotations from the Judaic Scriptures (the *"Tanakh"*) are the author's own translation or paraphrase, made by consulting Snaith, Norman Henry. ספר תורה נביאים וכתובים. 2nd ed. London: the British and Foreign Bible Society, 1982. This was compared to other translations and tools, including Green, Jay P. *The Interlinear Bible.* 2nd ed. Peabody, Massachusetts: Hendrickson, 1986. Also consulted was the Septuagint Greek version published as *Vetus Testamentum Graece.* Leipsig: Metzger and Wittig, 1879.

Quotations from the Christian documents are the author's own translation or paraphrase, made by consulting the Westcott and Hort text as found in Aland, Kurt et al. *The Greek New Testament.* 2nd ed. New York: American Bible Society, 1968. This was compared to other translations and tools, including the Nestle text as supplied by the NIV edition of Marshall, Alfred. *International Greek-English New Testament.* Grand Rapids: Zondervan, 1976.

Islam's holy book, the Qur'an, was thoroughly consulted through the popular version of Pickthall, Mohammed Marmaduke. *The Meaning of the Glorious Koran, an explanatory translation.* New York: New American library, 1953. Comparisons were made with Arberry, Arthur. *The Koran, Interpreted.* London: Oxford University Press, 1983. The main quotation provided in Chapter 14 is a paraphrase.

A portion of other literature read, referred to or quoted,

is cited elsewhere in these Notes. Various excellent historical studies were consulted, not all of them being cited. Likewise not mentioned in every case but scrupulously examined was the old translation of the twenty-seven books of the *Jewish Antiquities* and the seven books of *The Jewish War* as found in Whiston, William. *The Works of Flavius Josephus.* Philadelphia: Lippincott, 1856.

Preface

"**Heart of Gold**" is a song by Neil Young, Alfred Publishing Company, 1973.

...science and technology...often seem to reduce life... An influential book on this perspective was *La Technique* by the Christian scholar Jacques Ellul, which was translated into English as *The Technological Society* (1964). It seems to me that people whose outlook on life is limited to the so-called secular reality deny themselves much of the help, inspiration, encouragement and therapy of the noumenal or spiritual impressions. It is true that these latter experiences don't provide completely independent reliability and can sometimes be quite misleading, but the same is true of the theories and claims of technology and science. Both approaches have importance, and it is well to walk both the secular and spiritual paths.

"**History became legend...**" The quotation is attributed to *The Lord of the Rings* screen writer Philippa Boyens and is found in the appendices of the "Special Extended DVD Edition" of *The Fellowship of the Ring* by New Line Home Entertainment, 2002.

Chapter 1. The world of the epic

Because many names are mentioned in this book, I used italics the first time a particularly significant name was used. Most names that appeared only once or twice were not italicized.

In regard to the **High Power,** the most commonly used word in ancient Hebrew for the supreme good is *El,* with its derivative forms *Eloh* and *Elohim.* The root is generally agreed to refer to superior might or power, and is applied to gods and human rulers alike (e.g. Psalm 82 uses *el* and *elohim* to refer to the latter). While in English the word "god" appears to be related to "good" (German: Gott, Gutt), the Hebrew expression for the Supreme Being is basically "the Power."

In regard to the **Rival,** there is an ancient tradition that its place of exile was on Earth or under/within the Earth, so that just as heaven was above in the sky, so hell was beneath or deep within Earth. In the biblical book of Job, the Adversary says he has come, not from a distant fiery hell, but "From wandering through the Earth and going back and forth in it" (Job 1:21), and that view is sustained in the New Testament book of Revelation in which the Adversary, after being defeated in the heavens was "thrown out to the Earth along with all his angels" (Rev 12:9). There has usually been thought to be a strong link between Earth and hell, as the English poet John Milton pointed out; though he did locate hell way off in space somewhere, he noted the direct connection: "Hell and this World – one realm, one continent / Of easy thoroughfare" (*Paradise Lost,* Book X).

The **creative Wind** comes from the Genesis expression *ruach elohim,* "wind of powers" or "spirit of (the) great power," the creative force that gives life. In the New Testament, the sign of the Holy Spirit is described in similar terms of a great wind (Acts 2:2).

Many have commented on the difficulty of the fourth day in Gen 1:14-19, which is also the first day, at least in the 24-hour sense. The suggested solution of **the skies clearing** on that day seems to work as well as most others. The "day" here, however, as well as the other six creation days, I take to be a metaphor, used in a similar way in other Hebrew and Christian documents (for instance, the "day of judgment" – a time of reckoning; as well as: "with the Lord one day is like a thousand years" — i.e. God's time is different from human time). While of course, an almighty Creator could have made the world in six 24-hour periods if he wanted to do so, or even bring everything about instantaneously, Genesis does not rule out a very ancient Earth with a very long development.

The day of the tranquility or rest (Sabbath) became a central belief in Judaism and was continued somewhat in Christianity. Though few people have ever believed that the Creator needed rest in a literal sense, many still hold that a break of one day in seven and one year in seven is necessary for optimum human wellbeing.

In ancient cultures, the act of **naming** indicated authority or power over what was named, and the knowledge required to give an appropriate or prophetic name was power. The often-heard opinion that Genesis is against human knowledge has no clear foundation in the text but comes from a misinterpretation of the "tree of the knowledge of good and evil." In Gen 2:9, this was the second of **two special trees,** the first being called "the tree of life." In order to respect the Genesis account but also avoid the kind of concrete interpretation that would seem to give the two trees direct power over human life, I chose to give them a strongly symbolic meaning.

The serpent (*nachash*) also has power but is closely connected to the influence of enchantment (*nichesh*). "Dragon" comes from the Book of Revelation which calls the Adversary *drakōn,* noting its identity to the serpent of Genesis (Rev 12:9). The story of the temptation and fall is taken from Gen 3.

About **efforts to restore the old relationship,** in Gen 4:26 these began in the days of Enosh, the son of Adam's child Seth. The term **Sons of God,** in a puzzling paragraph of Gen 6:1–4, has exercised the minds of many. In recent decades some (Erich von Daniken and others) have seen in this passage evidence of a visit to Earth by aliens from outer space. The greater likelihood is that the Genesis text uses the phrase "Sons of God" to mean "godly men." Gen 4 has a parallel to **the fall of the offspring** when it follows the line of Cain, in which Lamech decides he has the right to have an extra wife, bears highly gifted children, and then further decides that he will not have to face justice for killing a young man. A widespread fall into arrogance is even more strongly suggested by the fact that the Genesis 6 passage introduces the presence of that great wickedness which was soon to be punished by the gigantic flood of Noah's time. The flood-related tradition about Nimrod is followed by Josephus in *Antiquities of the Jews*, I. iv.5.

Chapter 2. A unique quest

The notion that **Terach** carved idols is a long-standing Jewish interpretation (Midrash Genesis Rabbah 38) and is also the view of the Qur'an (Surah 19.41-48). The belief possibly originated in a reading of Joshua 24:2 where Abraham's father may be included with those who "served other gods."

The life of Abraham from beginning to end is found in Gen 11:27-25:10 from which the following quotations were taken ("I will bless you…" 12:2,3, "Do not be afraid, Abram…" 15:1, "Know for a certainty that your descendants…" 15:13–18, "the uncircumcised male child has broken the covenant" 17:14, "Look around…" 13:14–17, "I have sworn by the Highest Power…" 14:22–23). The Christian and Muslim documents are largely faithful to the Genesis account concerning Abraham, though there are some differences in Islamic tradition when it comes to the patriarch's relations with Ishmael, e.g. Abraham escorting Hagar and her son all the way to Mecca (Surah 2.125, 22.26). The Genesis account of Ishmael's geneology and the range of his descendants' territory is found in 25:12–18.

Chapter 3. Finding important themes

Though it is possible for a son to be uncannily like his father, it would seem unusually strange if the life of Isaac showed exact duplication of the life of Abraham. It is hard to escape the conclusion that **some of the stories about Isaac were confused** with those of his father, since the following incidents in their lives are virtually identical: (1) Abimelech and the wife

— compare Gen 20 with Gen 26:6–11, and (2) Abimelech and the well – compare Gen 21:25–31 with Gen 26:26–33. The relations between the grandsons **Esau and Jacob** are covered in Gen 27–33.

The highly significant **Shechem Massacre** is found in Gen 33:18–35:7, but the story's prominent role is not commonly noted by students of the Bible and has in fact been allowed to fade into obscurity in Judaic and Christian traditions. The present book traces the strong significance of this horrible event from the time of Genesis to Christ.

The poetic passage from the book of **Job** is taken from Job 28. I had previously published an earlier version of this excerpt in an issue of the broadsheet *Concern*, Peterborough, Canada, June-July 1989.

The story of **Joseph's life** is covered in Gen 37–50. For the historical identities of **Pharaoh and Potiphar,** I have been impressed with the research and arguments of Egyptologist David Rohl and have followed his findings generally. His most relevant views as far this section is concerned are found in chapter 8 of his eye-opening book *From Eden to Exile*. London: Arrow Books, 2003. The significance of Rohl's work and that of fellow scholars Peter van der Veen and John Binson goes far beyond our Chapter Three. Together they have successfully uncovered the error of the key point on which the time lines of the ancient Near East have been constructed by western scholars. When the correction is made in their "New Chronology," suddenly the Bible's events and names begin to line up with many of the findings of archeologists and historians.

Chapter 4. Qualms and instructions

The life of Moses from his birth to the giving of the Ten Commandments is found in Exodus 1–20. For the meaning of the name **Yahweh** I followed the traditional translations rather than more recent speculations around the verbal root *hawah*, some of which are unnecessarily philosophical and often Existentialist.

Scholars have suggested three general **Exodus** routes through Sinai: north by way of "the king's highway" along the Mediterranean, east through the wildernesses of Shur and Paran, or more traditionally, south along the coast of the Red Sea. It is the third and most widely-favored option that is in mind in this book. **The Ten Commandments** appear in Exodus 20:1–17 and Deuteronomy 5: 6–21.

Moses' **crucial admonition** is taken from Deut 31–33. Deuteronomy has been subjected to almost endless attempts to separate it from the Pentateuch (the five books of Moses) and give it a late date. The book itself purports to be "the words of Moses (that he) spoke to the whole of Israel on (the east) side of the Jordan" (Deut 1:1.).

Chapter 5. "We want a king"

The phrase "very meek, more than anyone on earth" is found in Numbers 12:3 and the serious temper tantrum, the cause of Moses being barred from the promised land, is depicted in Num 20:1–13. **The conquest of Canaan** is the theme of the book of Joshua, while the statement that the purpose was to "drive out the inhabitants of the land" is found in Numbers 33:53–56. **The twenty-one districts** in which Canaanites kept their property are listed in Judges 1. Joshua's notable **farewell at Shechem** is in chapter 24 of the book bearing his name.

Israel's **cyclic** existence in Canaan is described in the book of Judges. That book places **the massacre of the tribe of Benjamin** near the end of the Judges era though Josephus puts it at the beginning, shortly after the death of Joshua (*Antiquities of the Jews,* V.ii.8).

The life of Samuel is recorded in the first book of Samuel. He dies at the beginning of I Sam 25 and has no mention in the so-called second book of Samuel. The latter book deals with **the reign of David,** which is also covered in I Chronicles

11–29. Of **David's songs** quoted in this chapter are Psalm 57:4 ("My soul is among lions"), Ps 59:4 ("Though I did them no wrong"), Ps 55:6 ("Won't someone give me wings"), Ps 144:1 ("Blessed be Yahweh, my rock"), and Ps 110:1 ("Yahweh said to my Lord"). **The Song of the Bow** appears in II Sam 1:19–27 and is quoted from the lost "Book of Jashar."

Chapter 6. A house divided

The quotation that begins "Now in the days of your youth…" is from Ecclesiastes 12:1. The whole matter of **Absolom** is extensively treated in II Sam 13-19 and curiously escapes mention in the account of David's life in 1 Chronicles. The **manifesto** sung in the streets is attributed to a rebel called Sheba in II Sam 20:1. **Other songs:** "My goodness is nothing apart from you," in the third section, is taken from Psalm 16:2. "Yahweh is my shepherd" is of course Ps 23.

The birth of David's son **Jedidiah** is recorded in II Sam 12:24–25. He was the replacement for the baby born of adultery who had died at a very young age. **The life of Solomon** as king is covered in I Kings 1–11 and II Chron 1–9 and includes the claim that he sent ships westward through the Mediterranean Sea. The Phoenicians were already sailing with Solomon's ships south from the port of Elat towards *Ophir*, a distant gold coast whose location scholars guess at but which may have been in Africa (note the similarity in the names) — see I Kings 9:26–28. The westward journey, which was done only once every three years, possibly because of the great distances involved, is spoken of in I Kings 10:22 and II Chron 20–21.

The quotation from **the Song of Songs** is taken from an adaptation set to music, which appeared in an unpublished dramatic manuscript entitled *Greater Than Solomon*, composed in 1998 by the present writer. The story of **the life of Jereboam** (alternatively spelled "Jeroboam") is told in I Kings 11:26 to 14:19, and the acts of **Rehoboam** form a short interlude in that account.

Chapter 7. Prostitutes and prophets

James A. Michener, in his novel *The Source,* (New York: Random House, 1966) relates in popular style his well-researched findings about the sexual religions of Canaan. **The life of Elijah** is treated in I Kings 17–21, his death in II Kings 1–2. The contest on Mount Carmel and the prophet's subsequent flight to Sinai appears in I Kings 18. The prophet **Hosea** is known by the biblical book that bears his name. His wife and children are all mentioned in the first chapter of that book. "The prophet among you is a fool..." is found in 9:7, "they are the children of harlotry" is in 2:4, and the prophecy of Samaria's end as well as its eventual return to the land and to Yahweh is the message of Hos 3. The excerpt from a song by **Amos** is in Amos 5:2, the **Joel** quotation is from Joel 2:13, and "the fig tree" fragment is from Habakkuk 3:17–18.

The fall of Samaria is described in II Kings 17. The fateful reign of **Manasseh** of Judah is related in II Kings 21 and II Chron 33, while that of his grandson **Josiah** is covered in II Kings 22–23 and II Chron 34–35. The coming of the new **Babylonians** and the events around Judah's defeat and exile are briefly dealt with in II Kings 24–25 and II Chron 36. There is more in Jeremiah 39, along with the prophet's warnings in the chapters leading up to 39, and events under the Babylon-appointed Jewish governor Gedaliah can be found in Jer 40–43.

Chapter 8. Facing the death of the past

The first quoted **lamentation** ("All the people sigh...") is found in Lamentations 1:11–12, while the second ("By the rivers of Babylon...") is from Ps 137:1–3. **Jeremiah's prophecies** of a return to the land and the coming of a new covenant are succinctly described in Jer 31:23–34. His prophecy of the "Branch" is in Jer 23:5–6 and had earlier appeared in a prophecy of Isaiah (Isai 11:1,10). **The prophecies of Ezekiel** referred to in the present chapter are found in Ezekiel 11:16–17, 18:1ff, 36:16–28. His detailed description of a new holy land is in chapters 40–48. **Zechariah's prophecy** about "the Branch" is in chapter 6:12–13 of his own book.

For the works and sayings of **Ezra and Nehemiah** see the two books called by their names. Ezra's strong opposition to ethnic intermarriage is documented in Ezra 9–10, the Samaritans' desire to help build the temple (and Yeshua's refusal) is in Ezra 4:1–5. Opposition to Nehemiah's rebuilding of Jerusalem is noted in Nehemiah 4:1–8 and 6:1–14. Various Israelites add their names to a rededication document in Neh 9:38 and 10:1–27. Nehemiah frankly mentions his own harshness in 13:25.

The quotations taken from the book of **Malachi** are as follows: "I have loved you, says Yahweh..." Mal 1:2, 6, 13, 2:17, and "The Lord whom you seek..." 3:1. The reference to the coming of Elijah appears in 4:5–6.

Chapter 9. Brother against brother

The story of **Jaddua and Manasseh** is from Josephus (*Antiquities of the Jews,* XI.vii.2), and Jaddua's dream follows in XI.viii.4–5. The woman named **Niki** in our book is called Nicaso by Josephus who also mentions a Samaritan leader known as **Sanballat** in the time of the priests Jaddua and Manasseh but this is not the Sanballat who opposed the rebuilding of Jerusalem in Nehemiah's day, the span of time between them being two centuries, according to *The Cambridge Ancient History,* Vol VI and also www.historyofthedaughters.com, 2006. The second Sanballat strongly hoped that the marriage of his daughter would "be a pledge and security that the nation of the Jews should continue their good will to him." The first **Ptolemy** captured Egypt for himself and went to Jerusalem, took the city deceitfully on the day of rest and removed many captives from Judah to serve in Egypt (*Antiquities,* XII.i.1). **Antiochus Epiphanes,** his dealings with the high priest **Menelaus** and his severe persecution of Judaism appear in II Maccabees 4–7 as well as in Josephus.

The revolt of Mattathias is told in I Macc 2, the battles and reign of his son Judas Maccabeus in I Macc 3-9 and II Macc 8-15. The claim of Sparta about their ancestral link to Abraham is very dubious but is made in a letter of the Spartan king Areios to Onias the high priest, a copy of which appears in 1 Macc 12:19-23. I relied on Josephus' account of the life of John Hyrcanus in *Antiquities*, XIII.viii. The surviving queen who "divided the offices again" was Alexandra and her sons Aristobulus and Hyrcanus (not John) were the rivals. The whole episode, including the intervention by the Roman general Pompey, is in *Antiquities*, XIV.i-iv.

Tessa Rajak says (in "The Jews under Hasmonean Rule," *The Cambridge Ancient History*. 2nd ed. Vol 8) that "It is worth remembering that the tradition … channelled through I Maccabees, is dedicated to glorifying Judaea's Hasmonean rulers … The first book of Maccabees was probably written under John Hyrcanus."

Chapter 10. Voices of change

All the events of this chapter are taken from the four Gospels in the New Testament. The many brief quotations and allusions are to be found in those books of the Christian Bible, and what follows here are some of those references. The opening story of the confrontation with Samaritans is from Luke 9:51-56. The second account, involving the woman at the well, is from John 4:3ff. Details of the work and thought of John the Baptist are found in John 1 and Matt 3. Josephus in *Antiquities of the Jews*, XVIII.v.2 diverges from or adds to the New Testament's account on a couple of points, though these differences are of little significance to describing John's place in history as preparing the ground for Yeshua. The little sparrow illustration is found in Luke 12:6–7 and Yeshua's reference to the abuse of children is from Matt 18:5–6 and elsewhere in the Gospels.

The parable of **the Good Samaritan** is in Lk 10:30–35, Yeshua's views on the **temple** in Matthew 24:1–5, and the dismissive comment on **Nazareth** is from John 1:46.

The account of **the start of the ministry** is from Matt 4 and Lk 4. The "eye of a needle" quote is from Matt 19:23–26. "Give to Caesar…" is in Matt 22, Mk 12, and Luke 20, and "bringing a sword" is found in Matt 10:34. Yeshua's scandalizing of the "religious folk" can be found in Matt 9:11–13, Mk 2:16–17 and Lk 5:30–32. "If I expel demons…" is from Luke 11:20. "The Sabbath was made for man…" is Mk 2:27–28. **The primary commandment** appears in John 13:34–35, 15:12, 17, and I Jn 3:11. "You search the scriptures because…" is in John 5:39 and the "Son of Man" phrase appears first in the Jewish Bible in Daniel 7:13–14, while the quotation "Who has seen me has seen the Father" is in Jn 14:9–10. The significant passage that begins with "Come to me all you who are worn out…" is from Matt 11:28–30.

The account of **the Last Supper** is found in Matt 26:17–30, Mark 14:12–26, and Luke 22:14–23. The prophecy about "the rising and falling of many in Israel" appears in Luke 2:34. The memorable words "My kingdom is not of this world" appear in an exchange between Yeshua and **Pontius Pilate** in John 18:36–38. Further details on Pilate are found in Josephus, *Antiquities*, XVIII.iii.2.

Chapter 11. Questions and explanations

The **two disciples on the road** (to Emmaus) and the subsequent reappearance of Yeshua in Jerusalem is recorded at the end of Luke's gospel, Luke 24:13–43. This first book of Luke makes it seem as though Yeshua's last day on earth came almost immediately after the resurrection, but his second work (Acts of the Apostles) changes that impression: "He presented himself to them alive with many clear proofs after his suffering, being seen by them over the space of forty days, speaking things concerning the kingdom of God" (Acts 1:3). The "large group of over five hundred people" who saw him alive after the crucifixion is mentioned in I Corinthians 15:3–7.

The Feast of Weeks (Pentecost) account is in Acts 2 and **Peter's quote** from a prophet is Joel 2:29. The trial of **Stephen** appears in Acts 6 and 7, and **the conversion of Saul** in Acts 9 (which is testified to by Saul/Paul himself in I Cor 15: 8 and Galatians 1:13–24). His way of **connecting Abraham with Yeshua** is discussed by him in Gal 3:13–29 and Romans 4. Paul's humble estimation of **his weakness** is reflected in I Timothy 1:15, Romans 7:15–25 and II Cor 12:17–10. These passages show the Achilles' heel of all religion and idealism: the good is not attained because of the weakness of human nature which actively undermines the good.

The references to Paul's many acute distinctions between the present kingdom of God and the previous preparatory stage in religion are taken from various parts of his writings, including Gal 4:6, cf Rom 8:15–16, Gal 5:1, 4–6, 13–14, and Rom 14:17. "As long as God was true, everyone else could be a liar" is a reference to Rom 3:4. The phrase **apostle of the heart-set-free** was borrowed from one of many good studies of the life and teachings of Paul, namely Bruce, F.F. *Paul: Apostle of the Heart Set Free.* Exeter, UK: The Paternoster Press, 1977. The illustration of **Paul's inconsistency** to provoke an ungracious argument with close friends is described by Luke in Acts 15:37–39.

Chapter 12. The struggle to be

The warning about **the birth pangs** is in Matt 24. The smaller Zealot rebellions and guerilla strikes within the earlier years are discussed by Josephus in *Antiquities,* XX. **The First Jewish-Roman War** is covered in The Wars of the Jews II–VI. Essential details of **the Second Jewish-Roman war,** also known as "the Kitos War," were gleaned from the *Encyclopaedia Judaica,* 2nd ed. New York, Jerusalem: Macmillan Reference USDA and Keter Publishing House. Information about the

Third war, touched off by **the bar-Kochba revolt,** was provided by the *Encyclopaedia Judaica* and www.aish.com.

The early Christian creeds in Greek appear in a slim but prized old volume in my library as Heurtley, C.A. ed. *De fide et symbolo: documenta quædamnec non aliquorum ss. partum tractatus.* London: Parker & Co., 1889. **The Gnostic alternative** to this catholic view is inferred throughout the First Epistle of John, where their mystic view of themselves led the writer to call them "many anti-christs" (1:18), implying that Gnostics believed they could rise to the same spiritual state as Christ. Alternative accounts of the life of Christ became better known to modern people through the paperback publication by Pagels, Elaine. *The Gnostic Gospels.* New York: Vintage Books, 1981. She suggested that the appeal of Gnosticism in the early centuries of Christianity had much to do with a reaction to the fact that the Christian faith was becoming a matter of following a bishop of the church (as opposed to individual believers having spiritual knowledge), and she therefore used the term "catholic" almost pejoratively. She acknowledged, however, that Gnostic spirituality was a matter of "gifts" and therefore not equally available to all individual believers, and that it tended to produce extreme claims by some Gnostics that they possessed God-like insights and powers.

References made by **Eusebius** of Caesarea to forms of torture appear in his *Historia Ecclesiastica* (my copy: Parker, Samuel. *Ecclesiastical History.* London: George Sawbridge, 1703). His views on the age of persecution are generally considered more reliable than his discussion of Constantine, whom he revered. In later centuries, the church honored Eusebius only with caution, e.g. the Second Council of Nicea in 787 prohibited people from quoting him to prove the rightness of any matter, the apparent reasons being his refusal to criticize the Arians and his rejection of the cult of icons. *The Oxford Dictionary of Byzantium.* Oxford, New York: Oxford University Press, 1991.

The quotation "while the outward nature..." is from II Cor 4:16, "not worthy to be compared" is in Romans 8:18.

The source for the account of **Polycarp's death** is Eusebius, *Ecclesiastical History,* Book IV.

Chapter 13. The quest re-made

Constantine the Great inherited some of the religious pretensions accorded to Roman emperors during the Pagan era, as well as the ideas of some Christian thinkers about the relationship of Earth to heaven. This is discussed in the following excerpted essay which developed it for the period of the Christian Byzantine era ("Panayiotis Christou: the Missionary Task of the Byzantine Emperor" *Βυζαντινά, τ.3, Θεσ/νίκη* 1971, Myriobiblos Library website 17 May 2008): "Quite in accordance with their habit to look for analogies between things heavenly and things terrestrial, the Byzantines saw in their earthly empire an image of the Kingdom of God... And naturally the earthly king is a true image of the heavenly king. Besides it was from Him that the king derived his power, as the Byzantines were convinced... Constantine the Great confesses to labouring under a feeling of great responsibility towards God, arising from the belief that it was God who had invested him with ruling powers over all earthly things. He also declared his firm conviction that he was appointed and appropriately instructed by God for the realization of His will on earth."

The Trinitarian Controversy is discussed in numerous historical and theological texts. A brief yet scholarly treatment is provided by Gonzales, Justo L. *A History of Christian Thought.* Nashville: Abingdon, 1970. **The text of the law** that forced the Nicene faith on the empire is taken from Bettenson, Henry. *Documents of the Christian Church.* New York: Oxford University Press, 1967.

The story of **Pontitianus** appears in *The Confessions* of **Augustine.** A popular translation of it is published by Penguin Books, though our version was made by combining and slightly paraphrasing different translations. No doubt largely due to the nature of his conversion, Augustine understood the phrase "kingdom of God" in the Abrahamic spiritual sense. Though various emperors and popes have seen themselves as overseeing or protecting the spiritual kingdom, Augustine maintained a different view. He was apparently thinking of Abraham who "waited for the city ... whose builder and maker is God" (Hebrews 11:10) when he found a title for his huge work on a Christian philosophy of history, significantly calling it *The City of God.*

Chapter 14. The world after the epic

The Qur'an quotation "These are the limits..." is found in Surah IV.14–15. **The geography of worship** was a strong interest of Islamic society, the world being viewed as centered on Mecca and its Qa'ba (Kaaba), the cubic building that contains the material object of the sacred Black Rock. It has been important for the worshipper to be physically oriented towards Mecca and this made it necessary to have some map or guide, such as the Pole Star and a compass point in line with the Black Rock. The earliest known Qa'ba-centered geographic plan dates back to the ninth century (the third century of the Islamic calendar). This and several more are reproduced in *The Encyclopaedia of Islam.* New Edition. Leiden: E.J. Brill, 1991. The **Sufi** version of Islam receives a thorough and largely sympathetic treatment in William, John Alden, ed. *Islam.* New York: George Braziller, 1962.

A helpful tracing of the respective travels and influence of Judaism's **Ashkenazi and Sephardic** branches appears in Scheindlin, Raymond. *A Short History of the Jewish People.* New York: Macmillan, 1998. The reform ideas of **Moses Mendelssohn** had a surprisingly conservative core: he believed that what had distinguished the people of Israel was the unique law of Sinai. He wished to go back to the view of the great teacher **Hillel** (1st century BC) who was reported to have said, "Love thy neighbour as thyself, this is the text of the law —

all the rest is commentary" (from *Encyclopaedia Judaica,* Vol 14).

In regard to taking the sign of the cross, see Thorsson, O. ed. "Egil's Saga," *The Sagas of the Icelanders.* New York: Viking, 2000. **The well-known Roman Catholic writer** was G.K. Chesterton and his comment about the church's competitive position with the Holy Roman Empire appears in his biography of *St.Thomas Aquinas.* London: Hodder and Stoughton, 1943. The late medieval new lifestyles and modern personal piety for common people included the layman's "Devotio Moderna" in the Netherlands, the "Brethren of the Common Life" in the same country (with the related new spiritual classic called *The Imitation of Christ*) and also the "Brethren of the Free Spirit" in Germany.

Afterword

In regard to **the search as a discipline** "to prevent me from dwelling on my own spiritual experience and beliefs": though the process of discovery followed in this book did actually take place at a certain stage in my life, some aspects of it happened in earlier years. Various details about that relational perspective and experience were omitted because I thought it better for readers to discover some of these on their own. Relationships are personal, after all.

The parable is found in Matt 25:34–46 and was paraphrased in our book with reference to Matt 23:25–28. It is part of a series of parables and teachings by Yeshua in which he emphasized that since the present kingdom of God is spiritual-relational and not openly visible, people should guard against being swindled by saviors who promise an early coming of a glorious world. To Yeshua, the kingdom's full reality was for a later time in which he returns to bring about a complete and visible renewal.

About the author

Case Stromenberg comes from a Christian family that saved Jewish lives from Nazi destruction, a fact that spurred his no-nonsense approach to spirituality. The underground work done in the war was chronicled by his aunt Susan Stroomenbergh-Halpern in her book *Memoirs of the War Years: the Netherlands, 1940-1945*. After the war, family members emigrated to North America. Having studied in the U.S. and in three provinces of Canada, Case spent a number a years teaching history and religion, doing regular public speaking, and serving as mediator and counselor. During this time, he married and started a family of two children, published a manual for people caught up in religious conflict, and was a contributor to a college text on counseling. He now provides therapy and community support in the field of mental health.